Mister Rogers Talks with Families About Divorce

Berkley Books by Fred Rogers

MISTER ROGERS TALKS WITH PARENTS
(with Barry Head)

MISTER ROGERS' PLAYBOOK:
Insights and Activities for Parents and Children
(with Barry Head)

MISTER ROGERS TALKS WITH FAMILIES ABOUT DIVORCE
(with Clare O'Brien)

Most Berkley Books are available at special quantity discounts for bulk purchases for sales promotions, premiums, fund raising, or educational use. Special books or book excerpts can also be created to fit specific needs.

For details, write or telephone Special Markets, The Berkley Publishing Group, 200 Madison Avenue, New York, New York 10016, (212) 686-9820.

Mister Rogers Talks with Families About Divorce

Fred Rogers
and Clare O'Brien

BERKLEY BOOKS, NEW YORK

For the generous people who shared their stories with
us, and for Joanne, "J," Tory, and John, and Dick,
Kate, and Miles.

F.M.R. and C.O'B.

MISTER ROGERS TALKS WITH FAMILIES ABOUT DIVORCE

A Berkley Book/published by arrangement with Family Communications, Inc.

PRINTING HISTORY
Berkley trade paperback edition/October 1987

ISBN: 0-425-10350-1

A BERKLEY BOOK® TM 757,375
The name "Berkley" and the "B" logo are trademarks
belonging to Berkley Publishing Corporation.
PRINTED IN THE UNITED STATES OF AMERICA

10 9 8 7 6 5 4 3 2 1

Author's Note

A few years ago, several segments of MISTER ROGERS' NEIGHBORHOOD were devoted to the subject of divorce. The response from parents was so strong that I began to think more and more about how families might be helped through this trying time. Emotions run high during a divorce, and often parents, due to their own stress and sense of confusion, overlook the many ways in which they can help their children.

Reading has always had a special place in my life—not simply for what I have learned, but for the things it has helped me experience—and so it seemed that a book would be a good way to start to help parents help their children.

As you will see, much of this book has come from innumerable private conversations both my coauthor Clare O'Brien and I have had with parents and children about the problems of divorce. Some of the best insights have come from the children of divorce *after* they have grown up. All of those who have so graciously shared their lives with us, however, believe strongly that we can help one another when we share everyday as well as extraordinary experiences.

Those familiar with Mister Rogers' Neighborhood know that I have always tried to talk honestly with children about all the feelings that concern them. My wish has been to facilitate communication *within* families, to give families springboards for beginning conversations among themselves. The point is not to preach to parents about what to do or how to raise their children. Most parents are perfectly capable of deciding those things on their own. But I do think we can all benefit from the experiences of others who have traveled a similar road. So this book will not tell you how to get a divorce, but it will show how many parents have grown, along with their children, through their own times of divorce.

In spite of all the sad and lonely feelings, it is comforting to observe that many parents have developed strength and maturity through their experience and were able to transmit those values to their children. With love and determination, each of us is capable of growing through even the toughest times.

I'm sure you must be such a person. How do I know? Because you care enough about your children to want to read this book.

—FRED ROGERS

CONTENTS

SECTION I

THE DECISION
TO DIVORCE

CHAPTER 1

TELLING THE CHILDREN

FRED

Part of being a parent is having to do things that hurt a child. It may be something as simple as washing the dirt out of a scraped knee or something as difficult as breaking the news that a family pet has died. No parent can avoid times like these, and, of course, in bringing pain to our children, we bring pain to ourselves—pain of all kinds.

Some friends told me about a day when their ten-month-old daughter had to have stitches for a cut over one eye. As the mother held the baby's head and tried to calm her, the father had to keep the baby's arms and legs still. Their daughter fought against them, but the wound had to be stitched. "When we returned home," the mother told me, "my husband and I were wrecks. Neither of us could shake the feeling that it had been *us* who had hurt our baby."

Feelings like that must be as familiar to other parents as they are to me. When the hurt is an emotional hurt, and when parents and children are *both* hurting, the pain is

3

likely to be still more intense. I feel real anguish when I imagine two parents preparing to tell their children about their decision to separate. Here are two people trying to come to grips with their own feelings of failure about the past and fears about the future, and struggling at the same time with what they imagine their children's feelings will be. Many parents have told me how frightened and vulnerable they felt at that moment. Some have said they were so afraid of what the news might do to their children that they put off talking about separation far longer than they knew they should have.

Alicia and Joe decided to divorce six months before they were able to summon enough courage to face their three children with the news. Each time that they thought about breaking the news, one or the other found an excuse to put off the conversation. "You wouldn't believe how creative we became at avoiding telling the children," Alicia said. "First we wanted to wait until our daughter's birthday was over. Then we decided to wait until after the Christmas holidays. When our son began to show signs of difficulty with his schoolwork, that became the next excuse."

A close friend eventually asked Joe if he and Alicia had decided against a divorce. This question helped the couple see what was happening in their family.

"We realized," said Joe, "that we were looking for the perfect time. But there is no perfect time to tell or to get bad news. I don't know how I talked myself into believing that I could spare my children this hurt any more than my wife and I could be spared. A divorce is bound to hurt everyone."

CLARE

Alicia and Joe were fortunate that their delay in telling the children didn't cause more problems. Some children end up hearing about a divorce from outsiders and feel betrayed. They imagine that perhaps their parents didn't consider their feelings important enough, when, of course, it's really just the opposite that's true. In one family I know, a trusted relative was asked to tell the children of a pending divorce.

> "I don't think I will ever forgive my parents for the way in which I heard about their divorce," Kim said. "My aunt told me; the excuse was that my parents couldn't bear to hurt me, so they had Aunt Jill deliver the blow. Did they really believe I would be less hurt if they sent a messenger?
>
> "The funny thing is," she added, "I'm a grown woman now, and I still have some anger about this. I spent most of my growing-up years wondering what other bombshell they might be holding on to."

I can imagine the fear Kim's parents must have felt, but children deserve to hear the truth, no matter how difficult, from their parents, particularly if the truth is painful. The hurt caused by the news of a divorce is inevitable. That is one of the very sad truths about divorce. It is not a matter of whether to tell or not to tell, but rather *how* parents present the news of a divorce to a child that makes the difference. If parents are evasive or dishonest with their children, they broadcast an unhealthy lifetime message. But when parents face the truth honestly, they help their children grow into people who can do the same.

FRED

I've always believed that honesty is an essential part of trust between parents and children. For one thing, knowing the truth helps children summon the inner strength to deal with life's challenges. There's a song I sing on *Mister Rogers' Neighborhood* called "I Like to Be Told":

> I like to be told
> When you're going away,
> When you're going to come back,
> And how long you will stay,
> How long you will stay,
> I like to be told.
>
> I like to be told
> If it's going to hurt,
> If it's going to be hard,
> If it's not going to hurt.
> I like to be told.
> I like to be told.
>
> It helps me to get ready for all those things,
> All those things that are new.
> I trust you more and more each time
> That I'm finding those things to be true . . .
>
> I like to be told
> 'Cause I'm trying to grow,
> 'Cause I'm trying to learn
> And I'm trying to know.
> I like to be told,
> I like to be told.

One mother wrote me a letter about that song. She told me it helped her to remember to talk to her son not only about big things but also about little things, too. "I realized that Josh used his imagination whenever he didn't have the facts about something," she said. "Most times that was okay, but now and then it could be a real problem. One time a neighbor offered to drop us off at the bakery on her way to the hardware store. When it came time to get in her car, Josh made a terrible fuss. Much later, I learned that Josh took her words quite literally. He had imagined she would 'drop us' right out of the car!"

That mother knew her son well enough to know that Josh's "terrible fuss" had been uncharacteristic of him, and that something was going on that she didn't understand. If she hadn't asked him about it later on, she might never have discovered how literal children at certain ages can be.

I know one child who said his parents were going to get "lavorced" and thought that meant they were going to use a certain mouthwash together; Lavoris was the only word he knew that even sounded like divorce. When we talk with children about things we know they don't understand, it can be helpful to find a time to ask them what *they* think we're talking about—what they think our words mean. When we know what some of their misunderstandings and fantasies may be, then we can know better what they need to hear.

CLARE

Some parents assume that to be entirely honest requires that children be brought into discussions about divorce before a decision is made. Most counselors I spoke with, however, agree that children should be told about a divorce only when parents have made a firm decision. Unfortunately, the actual decision to divorce is often preceded by a period of conflict and emotional upset. If during this time children ask questions, as they are likely to do, they can be helped by a simple statement of truth: "Daddy and I are having problems getting along. We hope to work out the problems between us."

Rose is the eldest of four children. She remembers that the relationship between her parents had been unhappy for most of her young life; her parents had argued frequently and spent increasing amounts of time apart. One Saturday morning, when Rose was thirteen, they called Rose into their bedroom. Her mother began the discussion.

"Rose, your father and I are thinking about divorcing. We haven't been getting along for a long time and feel pretty sure the situation won't improve." Even though her mother's words didn't surprise her, Rose was totally unprepared for her overwhelming sense of panic. Her father continued, "How do you think Ed and June [Rose's siblings] would feel? Is Ed too young?" The more her mother and father talked about their concerns, the more upset Rose became. "I was sure if either of them said one more word, I'd burst."

"Of course, I told them not to do it," she told me. "What did they think I would say? My mother actually seemed surprised that I was so upset. I begged them not to divorce, and they promised they wouldn't. No one mentioned the word 'divorce' again for six months. That summer we all went to camp as usual. When we got back, we learned my father had moved out."

Twenty years later, Rose's memory of that frightening conversation is still vivid. A part of her still imagines that if she had said the right thing, or done the right thing, she somehow could have persuaded her parents to stay together. While this is a common fantasy among children of divorced parents, Rose's parents fanned her particular fantasy by asking her opinion, creating the impression, because they asked her, that they would do as Rose told them, especially since they promised her they would. It's tempting to make promises we can't keep when our child acts upset, but it's never a good idea.

Children such as Rose, who actually succeed in persuading parents to stay together, if even for a short period of time, are filled with an unrealistic sense of power. Those who "fail" to effect a lasting reconciliation, which is usually the case, can become burdened with overpowering feelings of guilt, which are sometimes carried into adulthood.

There are, of course, other reasons why children should not be told about a pending divorce until the decision is final. Most children will find the uncertainty of waiting unbearable. As for all of us, the anticipation of an unpleasant event can cause children the most worry. In those situations where the parents do work out their differences and remain together, the children will have suffered needless torment. For some issues, lengthy preparation can prove helpful to a child, but in the case of a divorce too much advance warning is likely to bring unnecessary confusion, loneliness and anger, and can hamper his or her eventual adjustment.

> Justin was given "periodic bulletins about the state of his parents' marriage." As he remembers it, "I was only seven years old. A lot of times I felt like I was standing all alone, out on the edge of a cliff. I kept expecting a strong wind to come and knock me over. You would think that having all that time to prepare would have made my parents' divorce easier on me. It didn't."

Justin spent a long time before the actual divorce living with the feeling that his whole world was in jeopardy. His parents' discussions, intended to help him develop strength, only created an emotional upset that left him feeling weaker. "I was exhausted from feeling nervous all the time."

There is no one, strict formula to guide us in our

discussions about divorce. And while too much advance warning can be detrimental, it is important to note that most children want, indeed need, a few days to talk with the parent who will leave the home. A hasty departure will often cause children to feel that they are losing that parent forever.

FRED

Talk about divorce is one of the most serious conversations parents will ever have with their children. Everyone needs plenty of time—not only for talking but also for crying and hugging and holding. It needs to be quiet time, safe time, private time.

CLARE

Divorcing parents sometimes feel so angry they find it difficult to resist blaming the other partner for all the problems. Several children I spoke with confirmed this. One woman expressed what seems to be a common concern of children in this situation: "How I hated hearing about all those problems! I never understood any of them anyway. As a child I couldn't stand to hear my mother's complaints about my father. I would tell Dad to help Mom with work around the house; then I would beg Mom to be nice to Dad. I believed it was that simple."

One of many reasons for parents to make an effort to be together, and refrain from ascribing blame, when telling the children about a divorce, is to present a united front and to prevent a situation in which a child feels pressured to choose one parent over the other.

> "The one thing I hated most about my parents' divorce, really hated, was hearing them tear each other apart," Mary Louise said. "If I'd believed half what they

said about each other, I'd have had to conclude that neither one of them had any good qualities."

Each of Mary Louise's parents spoke to her about the divorce separately. "My mother went through a laundry list of Dad's faults; my father took one shot after another at my mother. Why couldn't they understand that I loved and needed both of them?"

Mary Louise felt as if she was being tugged between the two people she loved and needed. After all, they were the only mom and dad she had. Because she believed that she was so much like both her mother and father, she often wondered if they felt the same way about her as they did about each other. These feelings were very painful.

FRED

Children who are forced to listen to a list of wrongs done by one parent to the other are almost sure to feel that they're expected to take sides. Siding with one parent has to mean turning your back on the other, and that may bring deep-down feelings of betrayal and guilt. Making children take sides can be a terrible burden for them to bear.

CLARE

Children are likely to feel more secure if they understand that the decision was made by *both* parents. If one parent is absent from the first divorce conversation, the children will wonder about the feelings of the absent parent.

Brent was eleven when his father took him out for a movie and pizza. "Right in the middle of a bite, my Dad told me he and Mom were getting divorced. I was really shocked. When I saw my mother later that night, I didn't know what to say to her. So I just said goodnight and went to my room.

"For the longest time, I couldn't figure out where Mom stood in this. Did she care? Was it just Dad's idea? Or hers too? I decided that Mom must not care about me very much; otherwise why wouldn't she talk to me about it?"

Brent told me it took several years before he could talk to his mother about his feelings, particularly his feelings of anger. Much later, Brent's mother explained that she hadn't joined the conversation because she'd thought his father would do a better job of telling the boy. Brent had imagined every possibility but the real one. His mother cared a great deal about him; yet Brent was sure she simply didn't love him enough to bother to be present when he was told the news.

Of course, there are times when one parent may be forced to be alone when telling the children about a separation or divorce. If one parent has abandoned the family or has a special problem, this also needs to be discussed openly. A child who is abandoned by a parent, either physically or emotionally, suffers a special hurt and will need extra support from the parent who remains as well as from other concerned adults. When one parent abandons a family, or is absent because of a problem such as alcohol addiction, it is very important to avoid speculation about possible reasons and limit conversation about that parent to what is actually known to be true.

"When Eve left six years ago, I had no idea where she went," Tom told me. "We had had plenty of problems, and I have to admit that I had a pretty big role in a lot of them. It has taken me a few years to realize that she bolted because she knew she could never get through to me."

Tom and Eve had permitted their marriage to deteriorate to the point where neither one could break through the rock-solid wall of anger between them. Racked by bitterness and frustration, Eve packed some things and left. She spent nearly one year in California, 3,000 miles away from her family, during which time she worked through her anger with the help of a therapist. In time, she felt ready to contact her family again.

Meanwhile, Tom and the children were making adjustments to a single parent household. The anger Tom had felt during his marriage only increased when Eve left. As the children struggled to understand their mother's actions, Tom cast her in the role of an irresponsible villain. Though he didn't know where she had gone, he created the impression that she was in some sort of paradise enjoying a vacation from responsibility. The children were left with the feeling that their mother had run away from *them.* A tight alliance developed between the children and their father. With only one parent in their lives, the children grew very dependent on Tom and accepted his view of the breakup.

"Our marriage was chaotic," Tom told me, "but Eve's return was a nightmare—especially for the kids. I could see they were torn between their deep need for her and the tremendous anger they felt."

"When I came back," Eve said, "I was prepared for an uphill struggle. The year in therapy had helped me understand myself and my marriage. My therapist and I spent months preparing me to face the kids. I knew they'd be angry no matter what Tom had told them. They were entitled to be; their mother had walked out on them. I wasn't even surprised that Tom had blasted me. Maybe I would have done the same thing in his place. Luckily, I was prepared to inch my way back in. Accepting the children's anger was the hardest thing I've ever had to do—except, of course, leaving them."

Parents in Tom's circumstance often find it difficult to contain the rage they feel toward the abandoning spouse. As his family struggled to sort out their lives when Eve returned, Tom learned a great deal about himself. After a good bit of effort, the entire family was able to talk through many of their problems. "My own anger about Eve had hurt the kids," Tom said. "I realize that now. I wish I hadn't pictured her as a woman without feeling who abandoned her children. She was really in pain and running away from her relationship with me. It took a long time, but a lot of healing happened for all of us. Even though Eve and I got a divorce, the kids know that they have *two* parents who care for them a lot!"

FRED

One parent may not always understand why the other left, and we certainly can't expect that children will understand, either. What we may be able to help them understand, though, is that *they are not the cause.* One father I spoke with said he left his children because he just couldn't face his responsibilities. "It was my problem," he said, "not theirs." Children need to hear and know things like that.

CLARE

When a specific problem such as alcohol, drugs or physical abuse is the reason for divorce, children will have already picked up certain clues. Because they have been living the problem, they should be told the truth. This usually works best if the explanation is made in simple statements. For example, if alcohol is the problem, one might say: "Mommy has a problem, an illness." Most children will ask lots of questions, but they need only be told what they can understand and what pertains to them. Parents often avoid talking with children about a serious problem, believing that this approach will spare them pain. Unfortunately this can backfire. There is always a danger that children will hear the truth from someone else and the parent will then have to deal not only with the truth but also the fact that they weren't honest in the first place.

> Mary's husband, Tim, was an alcoholic. After years of living through his unsuccessful attempts to stop drinking, Mary packed up their three kids and moved in with relatives.
> "There were months during which Tim was sober," she said. "At those times he tried to be involved in the family, and everything would seem to go along pretty well. Then, out of the blue, he would stay out all night and come home blind drunk. I covered up for him with the kids; I didn't want them to know their father was like this.
> "When he sobered up, he always gave me the same promises: he loved me and the kids; he'd never do it again. His story never changed and neither did the drinking episodes.
> "One time he stayed away for three days. I was frantic. Finally, I realized that unless I changed nothing would. I felt I had no choice except to leave."

Mary believed she was helping the children when she concealed the nature of Tim's illness. "I later found out that they really knew what was happening the whole time we lived together," she said. "What they didn't realize was that Tim had a disease he couldn't control. It helped them immensely when I told them that their father didn't choose to be the way he was. We got some help from Al-Anon, and I must say the whole family has grown a lot through this shared experience."

Every child, even a young one, can be helped to understand something about a problem that profoundly affects his or her life.

FRED

There's really no age at which a child won't be affected by a separation from his or her closest caregivers.

One mother told me about once having to take a two-week trip away from her baby who was only four and a half months old. "I was unsure about going," Karen told me, "but I checked with our pediatrician, who assured me that four months was an ideal time for separation, from my little daughter's vantage point. I was really surprised when I returned from the trip to find that she had actually been aware of my absence. She was so excited to see me that she kept holding my face with her little hands. For the next several days, she reached out to me whenever I tried to leave the room. It was only later that my husband told me she'd become really listless after I left."

At the beginning of their lives it's natural for healthy babies to feel that they and their caregivers are all one. Comfortable feelings of separateness come only much later, so forced separations in the early days are bound to be hard. In the sad instance when a divorcing parent no longer intends to have any physical relationship with a baby, or will have only limited contact, that baby may need extra holding and hugging from the parent who remains. It can be a difficult transition.

CLARE

In families where the children's ages span several years, parents frequently wonder whether they should talk to each child separately. Some parents I spoke with did that in the belief that one conversation with everyone together could never satisfy children of different ages. While it is true that a child's questions and concerns may differ with his or her age, all children in a family share one major concern: They will no longer be living with both parents.

Jeff and Rebecca had four children, aged eight, ten, sixteen and eighteen, when Rebecca became ill. Her doctor diagnosed a rare form of cancer that did not respond to treatment. As Rebecca grew weaker, Jeff realized that the children needed to be told more about their mother's condition. Believing that the eight- and ten-year-olds were too young to fully understand, he told the older children and urged them not to discuss it with anyone, particularly the younger children.

"I wish I hadn't done that," Jeff told me. "I thought the younger ones wouldn't understand or that they'd enjoy the last months with their mother more if they didn't know about her illness. Without realizing what I was doing, I had created a separation between the children at a time when they could have been a great comfort to each other.

"What was even worse was that the younger children could sense that something was wrong, but felt they had no one with whom to share their feelings. They felt scared, but were not clear about why. We were all acting differently, but they didn't understand the reason."

Siblings who face the loss of a parent, whether through death or less permanently through divorce, often grow closer to each other. The bond of shared grief can bring them to lean on one another for comfort and support. When parents talk to all the children as a group, no matter what the difference in their ages, they can help reinforce the basic solidity of the family. In the case of divorce, the point is that mother and father are divorcing *each other*, not the children.

Joel's recollection of his parents' conversation is vivid. One morning when he was eleven, Joel's parents sat on either side of him and his seven-year-old sister, Jane, and said that the family needed to have a serious talk. "For some time," his father began, "Mommy and I have had a hard time getting along. We fight more than we get along, and each one of us has been feeling sad much of the time."

"These sad feelings," his mother added, "have nothing to do with you. We've tried to get along better and do nice things for each other, but no amount of effort seems to change the way we feel about each other now." Tears started to fall down her cheeks.

"The one thing that has not changed," said his father, "is our great love for you, Joel, and you, Jane. We love you very much and know that you are the most wonderful thing that came from this marriage.

"I'm going to have a new place to live," his father told them. "I've found an apartment with a special place for each of you to sleep and play when you come to visit."

Joel's mother said, "Daddy and I will no longer be married, but you will still be *our* son and daughter. We love you and nothing can ever change that."

The way this couple handled the conversation with their children is impressive. They were together and shared both their love for the children and their sadness about what was happening. They also renewed their commitment to their children. Undoubtedly Joel and Jane were sad and hurt, but I'm sure that they each left the conversation believing that their parents loved them very much.

FRED

Each child who has to go through being told about a divorce is going to have a different set of feelings about it. Some will seem more angry than anything else. Some will be very, very quiet. Others will cry and cry and cry. Some will beg and plead for their parents to change their minds. When the parents of one child I know asked her if she had anything to ask about what they had just told her, she could only keep repeating the same questions again and again. That was her way of trying to understand just a little part of what was happening.

One man who was divorced ten years ago when his children were nine and eleven recalls that his children kept wanting to know the simplest things. "Where will I live?" "Will I still see you?" "Do you love me?" After listening to their questions he realized his children wanted assurance that he and their mother still loved them even though he and his wife no longer loved each other. It's common for children to assume that their parents can stop loving them at the same time their parents stop loving one another. It's as important for children to know that's not so as it is for them to know that the divorce isn't their fault and that there will still be someone to take care of them.

CLARE

The earlier parents are able to be specific, the greater security a child is likely to feel about the future. "I will be living at 1011 Elm Street; we can visit there tomorrow," is easier to accept than a vague reference to the noncustodial parent's separate living quarters. If no permanent arrangements have been made, it is important to tell the children about anticipated plans. Children will want to know that there will be a place for them wherever the noncustodial parent lives.

No one can write an actual script for the difficult conversation in which parents tell children of the decision to separate or divorce. Each parent must decide what is appropriate to the family's situation and then talk about it in his and her own special way. As one thoughtful mother told me, "I tried to put myself in my child's place. If I was seven years old and this was happening to me, what would I want to know?"

This mother learned a basic fact: All children need reassurance. As essential as the "first conversation" is, it can't be expected to cover every worry a child might have. As children mull over what we've told them, new questions and concerns will arise. Emphasizing that they're welcome to ask about anything that bothers them makes it clear that this is only the *first* of many important family talks about divorce.

SUMMARY

- All children need to hear and know that they did nothing to cause the divorce.

- The children need to understand that even though their parents have stopped loving each other, they will still have the love of both parents. Some children also need to be told that they are free to feel loving toward both parents even though those parents may feel angry and unloving toward each other.

- All children need to be told they will still be taken care of. They need assurance that one parent will not be lost to them forever because of the divorce.

- They need to be told the truth so that they may continue to trust both parents.

- They need to feel free to be sad and angry and to talk about those important feelings.

CHAPTER 2

TELLING OTHER FAMILY MEMBERS AND FRIENDS

CLARE

For most couples, telling their own parents of an impending divorce is as difficult as telling their children; feelings of guilt and failure are mixed with sadness and shame. Few parents take the news of a child's divorce without a great deal of distress, even if it comes as little surprise. It's a very normal thing for parents of any age to indulge in some degree of wishful thinking about their children's happiness. When a divorce is announced, they realize just how much unhappiness those whom they love have actually been through. And parents of divorcing children will be concerned about the physical and emotional well-being not only of their own child but also of their grandchildren. This is a natural response of loving parental feelings. However, because of their great love for their own child, at this sensitive time parents often side against their child's spouse without realizing that they may be doing so at the expense of their grandchildren.

Sally and Bob grew up in the same suburban Wisconsin town. Their families had a fine relationship going back two generations. The family joke had always been that Sally was the ideal girl—until Bob decided to marry her. Then Bob's mother decided he could have done better. "But Sally's really a terrific person," Bob told me. "She's a fine mother, creative and bright.

"When I told Mom and Dad that Sally and I were divorcing, Mom went on and on about how Sally had never really been good enough for me. I don't think Mom realized what she was doing, but she really tried to make Sally into a villain—which she wasn't."

Fortunately for the family, Bob was able to see that people who take sides in a divorce help no one. Bob talked with his parents at great length about his marriage. Finally, he was able to communicate to both his parents how much he wanted to preserve the relationship between his children and both families. "When your families live in the same town, you develop strong family ties," Bob remarked. "With all the moving and changing most people do these days, I'm not sure everyone could understand exactly what I mean. I didn't want my children to lose out on what I had had growing up—this close extended family—simply because Sally and I divorced."

Until she realized she was hurting her relationship with her own grandchildren, Bob's mother was aloof from Sally and her family. "Eventually," Bob said, "Mom understood that the children would always have a first loyalty to their mother, that when Mom acted cold toward Sally, she was only forcing the kids to take sides."

At the same time, as children are fearing the loss of their parents' love, they may also be wondering about their relationship to grandparents, uncles, aunts and cousins. Many children who have shared their experiences about divorce with me told me that divorce made them feel that the bottom was dropping out of their world. They even wondered who would still be their relatives. "Since Daddy went away, would his mom and dad ('Gram' and 'Gramps') not be my grandparents anymore?"

> Scott and Katherine visited with both sets of grandparents frequently before their parents' divorce. One paternal aunt, to whom they felt particularly close, took them on regular weekend outings. After a bitter divorce, the children's mother cut off all contact with their father's family.
> "I was torn apart by that experience," Scott said. "When I was with Dad and his family on visits, I always felt uncomfortable. I could never figure out why Mom thought they were so terrible. I'm nineteen years old now, and my relationships are not good with either family. I've spent the last ten years going back and forth between families, feeling awkward with both. Neither Katherine nor I have a particularly solid tie to either one."

Sometimes divorcing adults act as if two entire families are divorcing, not simply a husband and wife. If relationships have been close, these additional losses add to the hurt that children already feel and can make the transition time that much more difficult.

> "In the beginning there was something I had a hard time accepting," one mother recounted, "and it was this:

My divorce frequently requires me to set aside my own
needs for the betterment of my kids. My relationship
with my mother-in-law was one example. She's the kind
of person who always sees the negative side of everything. No matter what I ever did, she always found
something to criticize. When Frank and I decided to
divorce, I consoled myself with the fact that I wouldn't
have to see her anymore.

"When Frank got transferred out of town, his visits
with the children, by necessity, became less frequent.
All the same, neither my in-laws nor my children wanted
to cut back on the time they had with each other."

At first this was a bitter pill for this mother to swallow.
The children were so interested in maintaining the relationship with their grandparents that they persisted in
efforts to gain her cooperation. "I realized that the children
loved Frank's parents," she told me. "As reluctant as I
might be to admit it, those grandparents helped my
children over many emotional hurdles after our divorce.
I've learned to be grateful to them for that."

It's also true that grandparents sometimes require as
much reassurance as the children. They may need to hear a
son-in-law or daughter-in-law say, "You will always be the
children's grandparents. Nothing will ever change that
—not divorce or anything." Grandchildren can be the
"light" of grandparents' lives. Being separated from them
can cause enormous emotional pain.

Mrs. Sussman had tears in her eyes when she talked
about her son's divorce. "I know the world is different
now than when I was first married. We lived in a
community where everyone knew each other. When
one of us had trouble with our husband, a few of the
ladies would get together for coffee and cake after the
kids left for school, and we'd cry a little. If it was big
trouble, we'd eat two pieces of cake and we'd cry a lot.
But we never got divorced. One husband ran off, but

that wasn't divorce—that was a nervous breakdown.

"When my son told me he was ending his marriage, I cried for days. I worried so about those 'babies' who were eight and eleven. I was sure I'd never see them again. Well, I have to give my daughter-in-law a lot of credit. She included me in her family from the start. She and the kids kept calling; they visited; she invited me for their birthdays. They even remembered mine. In some ways, I have a better relationship with them now than I did during the marriage."

Mrs. Sussman's daughter-in-law realized that her children's grandparents were part of her children's roots. "The last thing I would want to do is tear a plant from its roots," she said. "In fact, when any of my friends divorce, I urge them to work out as comfortable an arrangement as they can with their in-laws. Everybody benefits."

CLARE

There will inevitably be some relatives who do their best to talk the couple out of getting a divorce; they do so only because they care so much. All they can think of is the pain of divorce, and they want, as much as they can, to protect the ones they love from that pain. What they haven't known or experienced is all the pain that led up to the divorce.

When Patty told her parents about her plans to divorce John, they were distraught. Patty's parents brought up every imaginable concern: The children would be deprived of their father; finances would be tight, they'd have to cut back on all the extras, and even some essentials; Patty would probably be forced to take a job. Their list was long and depressing. "I felt guilty and scared to begin with," Patty said. "My parents made me feel worse."

Patty's parents explained why their first reaction was to talk her out of the divorce. "I've always been Mr. Fix-it," Patty's father said. "If something goes wrong, I'm always the one who wants to patch it up. I saw the divorce simply as something to be repaired."

Parents just naturally want to try to "set things right" for their children. When they hear the mention of divorce, they may think it's the first time it's been considered. Some parents may feel inclined to step in, ready with a plan to mend the broken relationship. Just as we must talk these things through with children, so must we share them with our parents. As one woman described her discussion with her parents: "I had to be clear about the situation from the start: 'The marriage is irrevocably broken; no one can change that fact. We've tried over and over, but we can't put it back together. What I really need now is the love and help I've come to rely on from you.'" Saying something like that can be a real help to parents. Their role is clear and they *know* they're not being called on to "patch things up."

Parents of divorcing adult children may experience fear and guilt, especially if their family has never known divorce. Their immediate reaction is often a reflection of the panic they feel. And if adults as mature as grandparents feel panic about the possibilities of changing "permanent" relationships, it is not hard to imagine how young children will feel.

"It never would have occurred to me," one mother remarked, "but my daughter, Melissa, thought her grandparents would be angry with *her* because of the divorce. She was actually frightened to have that first visit."

> "The first few visits with my Dad's family were awful," Melissa remembered. "No one mentioned anything. Here we were, going through this terrible experience

and everyone acted like nothing had happened. It was horrid."

During one visit, Melissa asked her grandmother to see a certain photo album that had pictures of *all* the family in it. Her grandmother snapped at her, "Now, *why* would you want to do that?" Melissa burst into tears. To Melissa's great surprise, her grandmother cried too. Melissa said that they talked and cried for a long time. "We grew a lot closer that day because we understood that we were both losing something with the divorce—time spent together with *all* the family. But we realized that we'd gained something as well: the ability to share our sad feelings with each other. I think I could tell my grandmother anything now."

FRED

It's not the words that matter so much as the wanting to try. If you are part of a divorcing couple and have parents as well as children, you can sometimes feel a double sense of guilt. It's important to remember, though, particularly at this time, the gifts you have given the different generations: You've given your parents grandchildren. You've given your children grandparents. And there are ways that they can comfort each other that only grandparents and grandchildren know.

CLARE

Once the extended family knows about the divorce, it's important to relay the news of it, in a matter-of-fact fashion, to the friends of both the adults and children involved. One woman I spoke with told me that her parents didn't inform her school of the divorce, and so she spent the next half year of her life trying to keep it from her classmates. "It was a real challenge," Marilyn said, "coming up with reasons to tell my friends as to why they couldn't come over to my house to play. I was terrified they'd learn about the divorce if they were there. After a while, it just became too difficult, and I made fewer and fewer play dates. My mother noticed that I was alone a lot and, thank heavens, she contacted the school to discuss the situation. The teacher talked to me and let me see that it was okay for my friends to know. She reassured me that if anyone made fun of me—my greatest fear—she'd be right there to help."

Children often feel that a divorce has set them apart from their friends, that they are "abnormal." The accompanying sense of shame can sometimes be alleviated if their friends are included in casual family situations, such as dinners or an evening of television viewing. Gradually a child is likely to see this new situation as acceptable, and normal.

When talking to children about their fears of rejection, it is sometimes helpful to share your own feelings. Everyone worries that friends will reject them after a divorce. Unfortunately, some people do just that. It always hurts when someone disappoints us in this way. If this happens, we might talk about some of the reasons friends act this way. Most often it feels good to share our hurt with someone who listens and understands.

> "After we got through the ordeal of telling our chil-
> dren about the divorce," one mother of three young
> children said, "Michael and I barely had enough energy
> to deal with our own families. These talks can be
> exhausting—emotionally, I mean. I found myself avoid-
> ing friends, because I just couldn't face going through
> the story one more time. I guess I just couldn't think
> beyond that dreadful moment of getting out the first few
> words 'Michael and I are getting a divorce.'
>
> "Once I told a few friends, it was better all around. A
> person here or there disappointed me, but for the most
> part my friends were very supportive.
>
> "The children followed my lead. When they saw me
> avoiding friends and keeping to myself, they did the

same with their own friends. Skip, who was ten, began scrapping continually with his best friend. This boy was both a neighbor and school friend, someone Skip had been close to since nursery school days. It happened gradually, with an accumulation of small misunderstandings: Skip didn't want to play after school; his friend was hurt and confused by the way Skip acted toward him; and they each blamed the other for changing. By the time I was aware they had a problem, things had gone pretty far.

"It took some time, but I finally realized that Skip was fearful that his close friends, if they knew about the divorce, would change their feelings about him. Unfortunately, but understandably, the one friendship that was the most important was the one he cut off first. His fear was magnified by what he picked up from my own behavior.

"It took a while to work out the misunderstandings all the way around. I wish I had talked more with Skip. I had no idea he would take things the way he did."

FRED

Children often think up elaborate explanations for why things happen in certain ways, things they don't understand. I'm not surprised a child could imagine that a divorce was shameful even when his or her parents weren't ashamed of it. Sometimes, of course, parents *are* ashamed to be getting divorced. Some parents have talked with me about that feeling. When shame is real, I would expect a child to pick up on it. Children pick up so easily on their parents' feelings!

CLARE

Many younger children are concerned about how their teachers will react to the news of divorce.

> "I always liked going to school," twelve-year-old James said, "but after the divorce I felt weird. I know this will sound crazy, but I believed that Mrs. Conley, my teacher, would think I had made the divorce happen because I hadn't been a good son."

> Thirteen-year-old Kenneth was "afraid my teacher would feel sorry for a kid whose parents got a divorce and treat me different. I didn't want her going around thinking 'poor Kenny' all the time."

Kenny needed some help understanding that it was only natural for the people who cared about him to feel concern when his parents separated, that what they felt was sadness and compassion, not pity. With children who are particularly sensitive about extra attention, or feeling "singled out," adults should be careful to express concern without overdoing it.

Feelings of discomfort about seeming different in general are particularly strong for most children approaching adolescence. Divorce can intensify the feeling.

> "Sometimes when I walked down the hall to my locker," sixteen-year-old Michelle said, "I'd feel like every kid in the school was looking at me. If two people were in a conversation and one glanced my way, I was sure they were talking about me. I felt my parents' divorce put me in a spotlight, and I was very uncomfortable being there. I wanted so much to be normal, to be just like everyone else."

Jean is a teenager who believed her parents' divorce made her a "bad" person.

> "I always went with the 'good' kids at school, the ones who went to scouting or were in chorus. I was in junior high when my parents got divorced," Jean said. "I thought the divorce made me a 'bad' kid. I stopped doing things with my old friends and worked at getting in with the kids who got in trouble. It seemed to me that they wouldn't care about my parents' situation."

Jean's teachers knew her well and saw the changes right away. They tried to talk with her, but Jean backed away, feeling the divorce was singling her out with her teachers too. It took time, and the support of family and teachers, for Jean to understand that her parents' divorce was not a reflection of her worth.

Most teachers are eager to help their students work through any problems that affect schoolwork and school relationships. As one teacher told me, "I encourage parents to share any important change in their children's lives, whether it's a divorce, a move to a new house, or even a change in the child's room. All of these things can affect a child's life, and it helps me to know about them."

I think it's best to talk with teachers and close friends of your child as soon as plans about your divorce are firm. Letting them know will help them to help your child. The more information teachers have about your child the more able they will be to help circumvent problems.

A child's fear of seeming different, or the fear of being judged by his friends, should be taken seriously.

> "Sometimes kids can say cruel things to each other," Joe told me, "even the best of friends. My son told me about some boys on the school bus who were teasing him about the divorce. It made me so angry that my first

reaction was to make them stop. I then told him of that old saying, 'Sticks and stones can break my bones, but names can never hurt me.' He was quiet at first, but then said, 'Dad, names *do* hurt. They hurt a lot.'"

FRED

We all know that "names" do hurt. Teasing hurts. Taking our children's hurt seriously can help them accept their feelings as natural—"good" and "bad" feelings alike. Children often have surprising sensitivities, not only to being teased but also to being the one who does the teasing. One mother told me a story about her daughter being teased by a school friend. The teasing went on, and the girl stayed upset until one day her classmate said, "This doesn't feel right; I don't want to do this kind of teasing anymore."

CLARE

When teasing actually does occur, it is important to remind children once again that divorce is a grown-up problem. They did not cause it and should not feel responsible for it. You may need to ask a teacher, coach or school bus driver to intervene. A teacher could give a general talk about things said and done that might be hurtful. Most children would rather not hurt one another, but cruel things can be said and we all need to learn how to see things from another person's perspective.

Some people imagine that the prevalence of divorce makes it less likely that a child will feel he or she "stands out" from schoolmates. Just because someone has a number of friends with divorced parents does not mean she or he will not experience some of these feelings.

Each family member is bound to feel vulnerable, insecure, and unusually sensitive about the divorce. I think it helps everyone grow a bit more comfortable if sharing flows easily among family and close friends. Feelings tend to be particularly strong right after the separation.

SUMMARY

- Sometimes relatives, including the divorcing couple, act as if two families are divorcing, not simply a husband and wife.

- When parents can preserve contact with the families of each divorcing partner, our children will not lose the love and comfort of grandparents, uncles, aunts and cousins.

- Those people who have a role in our children's lives—teachers, coaches, neighbors and friends —should be told enough about the divorce so that they can be helpful to the children.

- Some children will feel ashamed or self-conscious about the divorce. It is important to talk to them about these feelings.

CHAPTER 3

EFFECTS OF SEPARATION ON PARENTS AND ON CHILDREN

CLARE

Divorce is a life crisis almost as profound as the death of someone we love. It's the empty feeling from the loss that seems to be so hard to reconcile.

Mary Ann, who divorced her husband after eighteen years of marriage, spent almost twelve months "thinking of my life in terms of *what I was not*. I was not a wife, not part of a couple. I was nothing. At dinner I would see the table as having one empty place. I guess I felt that half of me was gone."

Mary Ann had grown up in a community where none of her parents' friends were divorced. Nobody she knew had been divorced. The only picture she had of an adult life was being part of a couple. After her separation, she started to avoid her friends. She imagined that they saw her as half a person. Looking back on that time, Mary Ann realizes that she contributed to her feelings of loss by cutting herself off from her friends.

FRED

Earl Grollman is a nationally known family counselor rabbi and educator and a special friend of mine. He talks about the time of separation as "going from a we-relationship to an I-relationship." Even though many books and movies seem to portray women as having the greatest difficulty adjusting to being single again, the adjustment is equally hard for men. Both men and women must face a new set of problems totally unlike those experienced in married life —and face them without the support of a loving partner. When a divorcing couple has children, the adjustment can be harder still.

When I think about raising our two boys, I know those years were richer because I shared them with my wife. When things were difficult, I always felt better knowing that two of us were shouldering the responsibilities. Of course, there were times when neither one of us felt sure we had made the right decision about something. During those times I felt better knowing someone else was praying and worrying aloud with me. The happy times seemed richer, too, because they were shared, times like something they had worked hard to do. I'm sure that part of Mary Ann's empty feeling comes from remembering important times in her own marriage. There's always some regret in divorce no matter how sure a person feels about the decision. A time of feeling empty and alone is almost inevitable.

CLARE

One man wondered, "How anyone came up with the expressions 'carefree bachelor' or 'gay divorcé' is beyond me! All I felt was lonely. I had lost my marriage, my children, and my home. I never felt the least bit gay or carefree. The hours I spent away from work were so drab and unsatisfying that I often worked until I was too tired to do anything but sleep."

Special circumstances sometimes make these lonely feelings even more intense. Michael and his former wife, Elaine, agreed to a temporary custody arrangement that gave their twelve-year-old son eight months with his father and the remaining summer months and school vacations with his mother, who had moved 1,200 miles away to attend postgraduate school.

> "When Elaine agreed to have Eric live with me during the school year, I couldn't have been happier," Michael said. "But as the practical realities began to sink in, I started to feel overburdened by it all. I felt obliged to be both a mother and a father, as well as cook, maid, playmate and wage earner. No matter how organized I tried to be, things never ran as smoothly as I planned. Either there was no milk for breakfast or the spare carton turned sour. The job was so much bigger than I imagined," Michael recalled. "Eventually I got to the point where I thought I was doing a terrible job with everything. I felt I was ineffectual at work, kept a terrible house, and was a short-tempered and useless parent."

Even though Elaine's day-to-day problems were quite different, she had many of the same feelings Michael had—only she had them 1,200 miles away.

"The thought of not living with Eric all the time wiped me out," Elaine said. "What kind of mother has her child living 1,200 miles away from her? A *bad* mother, that's what kind." As a newly divorced noncustodial parent, she realized that "in one two-hour plane trip, I went from being a wife and mother to a nonperson. I thought Eric could have a more secure, stable life with his father until I was able to establish myself in a career, but the pain I felt from the loss of being a wife and a mother was overwhelming at times and clouded some of my efforts to begin a new life."

Usually one parent or the other must adjust to living day-to-day without the children. For most people that involves a lot of pain. "It's almost like an amputation," one parent said.

FRED

Divorcing families are usually very angry—each person in the family has his or her own hurt to be angry about. The part about it that's the scariest is the worry that the anger will get out of control. When we're very, very angry we're afraid we'll hurt even the people we love the most. Such a worry is always frightening, but during a divorce it can be terrifying.

"What do you do with the mad that you feel?" Those are words from a child, but they speak to a concern that all ages share. Many of us grew up in a world that wasn't the least bit tolerant of expressing anger—except by war—so when we feel anger, we wonder what we can do with it.

As one woman put it, "I feel so much anger that I'm sure if I let go of one little bit of it, I couldn't stop. I have this picture of myself ranting and raving. It scares me even to think about it."

I felt sorry for that woman. Not being able to "let go of

one little bit" of her anger was her way of holding on to everything pent up inside her. Letting go of normal anger—and there is a lot of *normal* anger in life—doesn't mean that we're going to be out of control. We might surprise a few people if we say how angry we are at times, but that kind of surprise hurts only those who refuse to listen to the truth. Our real friends and real family will respect us for not harboring the mad that we feel.

There's no way that children can understand all the "mads" that are involved in their parents' divorce. While they do need to know that people get angry feelings about other people, they don't need to be burdened with too many details.

> "When my husband left," one woman recalls, "I didn't know what I was doing. I was in such a panic, I imagined our whole life would disintegrate. Somehow I believed that if I could convince our son that his father had ruined our lives, he would not blame me and my life would be easier."
>
> This woman lost no opportunity to malign her husband. "Sometimes, I would find myself exaggerating a few minor flaws to make him into a villain. But now how I wish I could take back those words! Our son suffered terribly because of the way I expressed my anger. I'm still working to repair the effects of what I did."

A sign of that boy's suffering was his unruly behavior —behavior that a school counselor brought to his mother's attention. After several months of working with a child therapist, the boy was able to tell his mother how upset he felt when she said "mean things" about his dad. His mom realized she was hurting her son, not her husband, when she expressed her anger in this way. She finally got to the point where she was able to tell her husband how she felt about *him*, which enabled him to do the same to her. It wasn't pleasant, but it did begin an honest process of real healing in that family.

After our television special, *Mister Rogers Talks with Parents about Divorce*, I received many thoughtful letters from adults who wrote about the divorce of their own parents. Some of them mentioned things that happened over twenty years ago. One person wrote: "How I wish my parents could have seen a show like that! It's so important to encourage children to have a good relationship with *both* parents. My mother's constant, angry, negative remarks about my father only made me turn closer to him. From that experience, I've learned to really listen to my own children—not to tell them what I think right away but to hear what they feel first."

CLARE

The importance of talking about feelings was underscored for me in conversations with the teenagers who shared their experiences with me for this book. One boy talked about his father's unreasonable accusation that his mother "put him up to" saying or doing one thing or another. "Anytime I come up with an idea that my father doesn't like, he tells me my mother put me up to it. It drives me crazy." I asked if he had ever told his father how he felt. "No" was his answer. "He's too unreasonable. He wouldn't believe me anyway." I mentioned that I thought that I understood his attitude because as a teenager, there were times when I had felt the same way—so helpless to explain myself that I sometimes didn't even try. Together we decided that this was a common feeling among teenagers —all teenagers.

A few days later I heard from this boy. He seemed very happy to tell me that he was able to ask his father why he thought that his mother put him up to things. "Something came up about a place I wanted to go. Right away my father said, 'You don't want to go there, your mother put that idea in your head.' When I asked him why he always said that, he thought for a minute and told me he really didn't know. I expected any answer but that. Then we *really* talked. I said what I felt; he said what he felt. It was great."

Talk with others about feelings—theirs or ours—though often difficult, can be surprisingly revealing. This father was made aware of something about himself that was interfering with his relationship with his son.

FRED

Everybody is forced to grow in difficult times, and children can be truly giving and helpful, sometimes remarkably so, especially when they understand what's expected of them.

> "There were so many times when my children really came through for me," a divorced mother of three recalled. "They helped me more than I could ever describe. There's a 'sad' that you feel when you're getting divorced that's different from anything I've ever felt before. I knew I wasn't helpless, but I felt helpless. I knew I wasn't abandoned, but I felt abandoned. In many ways they let me know that I wasn't alone."
>
> Another divorced woman wrote: "I felt as if I was going through life wearing a wet raincoat. I could do what I had to, but everything seemed to take much more effort.
>
> "I had a particularly difficult time at work. I walked home the thirty blocks just to wind down. I guess it didn't help, because the minute I walked in the front door, I burst into tears. The kids were there, and I could tell they were scared to see me so upset. I really didn't want to worry the kids. They were going through their own rough times. I was determined not to fill their lives with grown-up responsibilities.
>
> "My twelve-year-old son said, 'I wish you'd let us help

out, Mom. There are lots of things we could do to share some of the work.'

"No words ever made me feel better. My daughter fixed me a cup of tea, and we all talked a long time about how we could make our lives easier. I told my children about wanting to keep them out of my problems. They reminded me that they didn't have to be told to know when I was upset. In the end, it was the kids who made me understand that we were all in this together."

CLARE

There are those, however, who find themselves right at the edge of despair. Despair differs from sadness in one important way; it adds a feeling of hopelessness to the grief. Those who despair usually feel that nothing is right with their life and that their situation will not improve.

Al returned to his apartment one evening to find it emptied of everything but the clothing in his closet. His wife had taken their young daughter and moved to a destination kept secret by her family. Al had no news about them for several months.

Al moved back home with his parents for a while. After initial feelings of shock and sadness, he grew quite depressed. In a few months he had lost quite a bit of weight. He withdrew into himself more and more. "Some days I felt I had no reason to get out of bed in the morning," he told me. "So I didn't." Al's parents would plan things that included him, but for Al the effort to do anything was usually too much. Most often he preferred to stay home in bed.

This prolonged sadness worried everyone. After a talk with the family doctor, Al's mother approached her son about a counselor recommended by the family physician. "In the beginning I saw this shrink because of my parents. I knew they were worried about me," he said. "I'd been in their house for six months acting half dead, and they were scared. I could tell they were petrified, and I felt sorry for them.

"The first few visits were very difficult. All I did was talk about my parents or my job. But some time during my fourth visit, some thought made my eyes fill with tears. I don't even remember what it was, but I suddenly sat very still. When the doctor asked what I was thinking about, I bawled. I mean I cried like I had never cried in my whole life, maybe for twenty minutes without stopping. After that, I started to talk. I mean really talk."

FRED

To some people the notion of seeing a psychiatrist or psychologist is a sign of weakness. This feeling is usually a carryover of old attitudes from previous generations. Just because a person consults a "doctor of feelings" doesn't mean that person is crazy or weak. On the contrary! I think that asking for help when it's needed is a sign of courage and strength. Help can come from a friend, a relative, a doctor or a clergyman—anyone we can trust with our feelings. A person can grow enormously through sessions with a psychiatrist. Professional helpers outside the conflict can help us to face our anger and loss and to gain strength through the acceptance of our feelings. Therapy may not change a marriage, but it can help us leave behind old behaviors from the past as we try to establish new patterns for the future.

CLARE

Everyone who goes through a difficult time has a unique inner timetable for recovery. Troublesome feelings seem to be strongest in the beginning; with time, those feelings begin to feel more manageable. For some people it takes a long, long time to work things out, but just knowing that things *will* get better can at least keep optimism alive.

People who cope best after a divorce seem to be those who, after a while, were able to accept all their feelings and use the best of the past to create a foundation for the future. As one man said, "It takes a lot of time, patience and understanding to come to grips with a divorce. Looking back, I know I said and did things I shouldn't have, but I did some fine things, too. I know I love my kids more than anything, so I'm going to keep moving forward. It's the only direction to go."

When I heard that, I kept thinking of the great capacity we have for growth even when times are hard. "I know I love my children more than anything," this man says. Through this love, he finds the strength to grow.

SUMMARY

- It is natural and almost inevitable for the members of a separating family to have feelings of emptiness and loneliness.

- Children, while they need to know that people have angry feelings about other people, should not be overly burdened with the details of what caused that anger between parents.

- A parent, no matter what his or her personal feelings, should encourage children to have a good relationship with the other parent.

- The time of divorce, for all its heartaches, can still be used as a time of learning and personal growth.

CHAPTER 4

EFFECTS OF SEPARATION ON PRESCHOOL CHILDREN

FRED

Every child is unique, and each child will react to divorce in his or her own way. Three children in the same family may have very different responses because they'll be at different stages of development and have different temperaments. That doesn't mean, though, that they won't have shared feelings. In fact, divorcing parents frequently told me how surprised they were to find that their children's feelings were similar to their own.

One father, like many others, remembers the period following his divorce as a grim time. For months he felt listless and depressed. It took all of his energy to complete a day's work. He remembers telling a friend, "A good day was when I didn't feel perfectly awful." Although he wasn't aware of his five-year-old son's feelings at the time, weekend visits during that period were somber. They sat around watching television. Both slept a lot.

After a number of months, the father felt the need to pack those visits with activity—more than either could really enjoy, and as he ushered his son from zoo to lunch, to movie, to park, to museum, the boy seemed full of tension and nervous activity, too. Later, he realized they were both going through the same stages: first, great sadness, then the need to make everything seem extra-normal even though both knew so much had changed.

Loss was something they both shared—the loss of an important always-there person and the loss of the "family" as they had known it. As for feelings and responses, it was natural that some would be shared just as well as others would be unique to each of them.

CLARE

Many young children don't understand or don't know how to express their feelings. They often need adults who are willing to patiently "listen" to both words and actions.

When my husband and I adopted our infant daughter, I called the doctor who was to become our family pediatrician. We wanted some practical information about feeding and caring for a newborn. After answering several questions, the doctor wished us well and said, "Take a few days to get to know each other. Listen to your baby. She'll tell you everything you'll need to know."

I don't think I've ever gotten better advice from anyone. "Listen to your baby." I've been doing that ever since, and my daughter has told me more than any child-care manual ever could.

I think of this advice often, and find it has many applications throughout your child's early years. It is important, I think, for parents to listen particularly closely when a child's words don't come easily.

Jimmy was three and a half when his parents separated. His father had a Sunday ritual of taking Jimmy to church, then out for an ice cream cone. The man at the soda fountain always gave Jimmy some crackers and stale bread to feed to the ducks at a nearby pond. Both father and son looked forward to this time together.

When Jimmy's parents told him of their plans to separate and that his father wouldn't be living at home anymore, Jimmy cried. After a few minutes, he asked, "Who will buy me ice cream? What will happen to the ducks?" Both parents were surprised at how trivial his concerns seemed. How could their son worry about ice cream and ducks at a time like this?

But, to Jimmy, ice cream and feeding the ducks meant time spent with his dad. He was wondering what would happen to all of those times—and what would happen to his dad, too.

FRED

When small children experience hard times, they often express very big concerns in a seemingly trivial way. This doesn't mean that their worries are small; it simply means that they don't have the words to describe the depth of their worry. Preschool children often imagine that a parent who leaves the house will disappear forever. Any kind of separation from a parent can be scary for children. Even a child's first tentative steps away from the mother can be filled with wondering: Will we be too far apart? But divorce is not a voluntary separation for most children, so many children can feel angry in addition to feeling frightened.

One mother we talked with was upset by her four-year-old daughter's reaction: "After my husband and I labored over how we would tell Suzanne about our divorce, all she wanted to know about was her birthday party, which was a full six months away. I couldn't believe we'd raised such an insensitive child." That mother understood afterward that

Suzanne wasn't insensitive at all; she was expressing concern about her future. She may have been wondering if there would be any future at all! It's hard for young children to think of a life without both parents, and as they try to imagine that possibility, their feelings may come out in concerns about details: "Will I still go to nursery school? Who will take me to the park? Will Mike still be my friend? Can I go over to Grandpa's house? Who will cook my dinner?"

Parents of preschool children need to know that their children's worries can be greater than their ability to describe them.

CLARE

At young ages, it is entirely normal for children to believe that whatever happens in the world has some exclusive relationship to them. Remembering this helps parents to understand seemingly self-centered reactions.

Edra's father liked her hair worn braided down the center of her back. He told her it reminded him of his Swedish grandmother, a woman he greatly admired. One time, when she was four years old, Edra experimented with scissors on her long hair, cutting a big hunk out of one side. Her mother had to trim the rest of Edra's hair to match the part she had cut.

When Edra's parents divorced one year later, Edra became preoccupied with the idea that because she had cut her hair her father no longer wanted to live with her and so left. She felt terribly guilty about causing the divorce, though she never shared this concern with either of her parents.

In time, Edra became very concerned with how she looked, believing a certain dress or new barrettes might bring her father back home. Both parents noticed Edra's unusual concern about her appearance, but simply assumed that was typical of girls her age. To Edra the fact that her efforts went unnoticed by her father—he did not move back—made her more anxious and upset.

Often children keep these kinds of thoughts to themselves. They create, as did Edra, private dramas in which they plan to win back the parent who went away. Usually, the plans are built around some thing or some event about which a child feels guilty. That these feelings must be kept so closely guarded indicates their magnitude.

One way for parents to help young children talk about what troubles them is to ask open-ended questions: "Why do you think Mommy moved away?" is more likely to draw out the child's inner belief than "Do you think Mommy moved away because she didn't like to keep house?" The first question allows the child to say what he or she thinks. The second gives a possible—and possibly distorted —reason to which the child can only agree or disagree.

Edra was twelve years old (eight years after the divorce) before she told her mother what she had believed about her hair. By that time she had carried the burden of guilt for the divorce for so long that her feelings were deeply entrenched. Imagine how much more difficult it was to help Edra let go of her fears after so much time had elapsed.

Frequently, a child will think that an angry thought or wish actually caused a teacher to get sick or a friend to fall down. Conversely, he or she will believe that the same magical thinking has "power" to make good things happen.

At seven Seth was an avid baseball fan, so when a classmate invited him to a Yankee-Red Sox game, he was thrilled. Seth's parents reminded him that the family had promised to attend a birthday celebration for his grandfather on the day of the game. Seth was furious. First he tried to persuade his parents to go without him.

When that didn't work, he tried to get his grandmother to change the party to another day. All of his efforts failed.

On the day of the party, Seth woke up to heavy rain, which lasted throughout the day. His classmate got rainchecks and so, on the rain date, both boys were able to attend the ballgame. At breakfast Seth told his parents, "I'm really glad the Red Sox changed the day of the game when I couldn't go."

FRED

We know, as adults, that wishes don't make things happen, but it takes children a long time to understand that just because you wish for something doesn't mean that it is going to happen.

We often deal with this magical kind of thinking on *Mister Rogers' Neighborhood*. In one song, I sing about how wishes don't make things come true.

Wishes Don't Make Things Come True

One time I wished that a lion would come
And eat up my house and my street.
I was mad at the world and I wished that the beast
Would stomp everything with his big, heavy feet,
And eat everything with his big, sharp teeth,
And eat everything with his teeth.

But that wish certainly didn't come true
'Cause scary, mad wishes don't make things come true.

One time I wished that a dragon would come
And burn up my daddy's big store.
I was angry with him 'cause I wanted to play,
And my daddy just went to his store right away.

I wished that the dragon would burn his store.
I wished it would burn Daddy's store.

But that wish certainly didn't come true
'Cause scary, mad wishes don't make things come
true.

I'm glad it's certainly that way, aren't you?
That scary, mad wishes don't make things come true.
No kinds of wishes can make things come true.

CLARE

Magical thinking can be a powerful force in a young
person's view of the world. It imbues strong wishes with
tremendous importance. A child will often wish to have
one parent all to himself or herself, even to the exclusion of
the other parent. If anyone or anything interferes with this
desired exclusive relationship with a parent, the child may
feel very angry.

> Jordana's brother was born when she was three and a
> half. One day, her mother overheard Jordana singing to
> the new baby. Her tones sounded so warm and loving,
> the words seemed incredible: "I used to have a brother,
> but now he's gone away. I used to have a baby, but now
> he's dead."

All parents with more than one child have lived through
the upheaval that a new baby brings. The older children
fear their parents won't love them anymore, or will love
them less, now that the new baby is there, so they often try
to wish the baby away. Losing love, even just imagining it,
causes pain for all of us, at any age.

Children can also be jealous of the attention parents pay
to each other. If parents separate or divorce during this
time, the intensity of these jealous feelings may make a

young child believe that this jealousy *caused* the separation or divorce; "I wanted to be rid of Daddy—and now he's gone!" Immediate reassurance that the divorce is a grown-up issue can be very helpful to the distressed child.

FRED

One mother told me that she reminded her daughter "a million times" that she had nothing to do with the divorce. "Still," that mother told me, "my daughter wrote in a composition years after the divorce that her parents divorced because, when she was little, she cried so much. Not only did she have nothing to do with the divorce, our little girl had been a gurgling, happy baby who rarely cried."

It can be frustrating when we try our best and still our children don't seem to understand. One father said of his son: "He refuses to understand. I'm sure he doesn't listen to one word I say." That father had probably struggled over and over to make something clear to his boy, but the power of that little boy's wishes was simply greater than his ability to understand what his father was telling him. At moments like that it may help to remember how many times it took to teach the same child not to touch a hot stove or write on the walls. Being a parent takes great patience—and more patience than ever when you're going through a divorce!

SUMMARY

Sometimes our children react in ways that worry us, but it helps to remember that most of these are quite normal. Preschool children of separating or divorcing parents experience some or all of these reactions:

- Most children go through a time of great sadness. They grieve the loss of one parent and the loss of the family as they knew it.

- Young children often don't understand or don't know how to put their feelings into words.

- Very young children sometimes express their fears in the most basic terms: "Who will feed me? Where will I live?"

- Preschoolers are most likely to believe that Mom or Dad left because of some wrong they had done.

- The preschool child's greatest anxiety during a divorce is that he or she will lose the love of one or both parents.

- The most effective way to learn what your child is really feeling is to ask open-ended questions (such as "Why do you think Mommy and Daddy are getting a divorce?") that are likely to draw out the child's inner thoughts.

CHAPTER 5

EFFECTS OF SEPARATION ON PRETEENS

CLARE

Children between the ages of seven and twelve do not usually have the same distortions about the divorce of their parents that younger ones have. Nevertheless, they too can be expected to have very strong reactions. Many school-age children can listen to and understand adult ideas, but the stress of the family breakup can make them revert to childish behavior.

At eleven, Stuart was settled into a comfortable routine of school and sports activities. Like many children his age, he spent most of his time with his own friends. When his parents separated, Stuart's father, believing it would make the boy feel better about the situation, told Stuart he would be "the big man now."

The boy took his father's words literally. He was the oldest child, he thought, so, of course, he must now take care of things. The responsibilities Stuart imagined terrified him. He was particularly frightened at night.

Could he really protect his family? What if somebody broke into the house? Suppose his mother got sick?

The pressures eventually led Stuart to sucking his thumb and wetting his bed, habits he had given up many years before.

Parents can help children by keeping the lines of responsibility very clear; grown-ups take care of grown-up problems. For Stuart, the expectation that he take charge was direct, but parents should be aware of the messages they convey by their behavior and attitude.

After his parents' separation, Jim recalls having a terrible time coping with his mother's pain. She cried frequently and questioned her ability to do the simplest things. Jim, even though he was only eleven, decided that the way to get the family back on firm footing was for him to take charge. He imagined that his mother would feel better if he did the things she couldn't seem to manage. Before long, Jim was doing everything. He woke his sisters in the morning and got them to school on time with packed lunches; he checked their homework; he cooked meals. Jim's mother still felt very sad and helpless.

All went reasonably well for a while, but soon the excessive responsibility took its toll, and Jim's schoolwork began to suffer. His mother was forced to take back her responsibilities but Jim told us it was years before he could get over the feeling that he had let her down.

FRED

When divorcing parents can bring themselves to express their own feelings, they help their children begin to do the same. I talked with children who believed they could somehow lessen their parents' sad feelings. Many told me how terrible they felt when they found they couldn't. One girl asked me, "What good am I? I can't even make my mother happy." It might have helped her to hear that her parents loved her and that they knew she loved them. Parents can't make children happy all the time, and children can't make parents happy all the time. Happiness has to come from inside a person. Relieving children of the burden of "fixing" their parents' lives leaves them free to feel their own sad and angry and happy feelings and can make it easier for them to adjust to the changes in their lives.

Another aspect of taking on adult responsibility is reflected in the enormous efforts preteens have been known to make toward bringing back the parent who has left.

CLARE

Kerry was twelve when her parents separated. She was the youngest of three children and the only one remaining at home. She devoted every waking thought to devising a plan to get her father back home. "When he visited on Sunday I would have all his favorite foods for dinner," she told me. "I was convinced that if I could get him to stay until ten o'clock, it would be easy to get him to stay overnight.

"When that didn't work, I wrote and directed plays for children in the neighborhood. They were always scheduled for the evening so I could convince him to come after work. When it got late enough, I'd suggest he stay overnight.

"A few times I was successful in getting him to sleep over and take the train to work the next day. Eventually," she said sadly, "I realized that he would not be back for good.

"Even so, I wasn't ready to give up. I decided that if I was very sick, he'd have to come home. I made up more symptoms than the bubonic plague. As I think back on it now, it must have been pretty funny: pains that moved from belly to limb, dizziness, headaches, chills. You name it, I had it. What finally gave me away was a temperature of 110 when I kept the thermometer in hot water too long. I didn't know about the normal limits of body temperature then. Even though it has become kind of a family joke, I still feel a little sad when I'm reminded of it. I've never wanted anything so much in my life."

Other children talked of their extraordinary efforts to get a parent to return home, from promises to never be bad again to running away from home. This phase usually passes quickly, particularly when parents make it clear that their separation from each other is as permanent as is their love for and commitment to the child; nevertheless, for children who have known the earliest love of a mother and a father it's only natural that those children might hold on to a wish for their parents' reconciliation for years—maybe way down deep forever.

Sometimes symptoms of illness are deliberately made up, as in Kerry's case, but it should also be remembered that the stresses of a changing family situation and the loss of a parent can give rise to actual physical ailments such as headaches, stomach aches, and fever. It is important that illness not be automatically dismissed and that communication of feeling be encouraged.

FRED

Some children talked to me about how they avoided feeling *anything* because their hurt from the divorce was so great.

"The year before my parents divorced we took a trip out West," one girl recalled. "All during the divorce, I would think about the Hoover Dam. To me, my feelings had the power of all that water, and if I didn't hold back the feelings, they would destroy something.

"After the divorce I was reading *Little Women.* Every time I got to a part that reminded me of the way the four girls stuck together, I would feel such pain, I'd cry and put the book away. A year later I tried reading the book again. This time I got as far as the reunion of the girls with their father and that made me so sad I put the book away again. I was in my twenties before I read that book to the end. It may sound silly, but I consider finishing *Little Women* a milestone."

As an afterthought she added, "In case you're wondering, even at twenty-two I couldn't get through reading it without crying at the sad parts, but I think that's okay."

Just as preteen children are coming to feel in control of some feelings, they are also forming a set of beliefs about what is "right" and "wrong." All of the limit-setting parents have been providing begins to show up as *self*-discipline during these years, and children often begin to express strong views about what they believe to be fair and just. "All my lessons are coming back to haunt me," one father remarked. "My son tells me what's fair about this or what's right about that. The other day, I was angry with a repairman who failed to show up for the third day in a row. I muttered something about his being lazy. The next thing I knew my son was giving me a lecture about being unkind!"

CLARE

Several divorcing parents of children who were between nine and twelve described their children's reactions as stern and judgmental. "How could you have done such a thing! Divorce is wrong!" Nobody likes to be judged, and at this time parents are usually feeling guilty enough as it is. The wagging finger of judgment, especially coming from our own children, can hurt a lot.

In response to an angry outburst of his child, one father said, "Your mother and I worked hard to make our marriage satisfying, but we weren't able to be happy together. Our divorce hurts you but it hurts us, too. We wish it didn't happen, and neither one of us did anything purposely to make it happen." Then he said something very thoughtful: "You know I care about how you think about me. I really do. That's why I want to talk with you about things—even the toughest things." Such a message will serve that child—and that father—well for all of their lives.

A few children told me about having very angry feelings toward one parent, who he or she believed was responsible for the divorce. It is difficult for children at this age to understand how complicated adult relationships can be and they often have very clear-cut beliefs about who is right and who is wrong. Naturally the parent who is cast as a villain in the child's eyes can feel very hurt.

> "When I remember how I treated my father after my parents separated, I cringe," Ricky told me. "We were five children, but the three oldest are twelve years or more older than I am. My brother Don and I were like a second family. There were always lots of problems between my parents, but Mom was the one who moved out. She wanted to try something completely different without the responsibilities of a house or kids. She even moved into an apartment that didn't allow dogs or children. The place had a pool, but we couldn't go in unless nobody else was there."
>
> Ricky and Don stayed with their father, who managed the house, performed his job and handled a complicated schedule of the boys' school and sports activities. "I was furious when my parents quit on their marriage. And I missed my mother so much I couldn't stand to think about it. It was the first time I felt a sadness that didn't go away. So I got mad at Dad. I criticized his cooking. If he was one second late for something I yelled at him. I cursed, I told him he was stupid, I said really horrible things."

When children direct their anger at one parent, it causes that parent a lot of concern and worry. It hurts anyone to be the victim of angry outbursts, but when they come from someone we love, the pain can be particularly difficult.

Ricky's dad found a way to help the whole family through this difficult time. He sat down with both boys and shared with them his own feelings about the divorce. He told them he wanted things to go smoothly at home but wasn't able to be responsible for keeping *everybody* happy and would never be able to make *everything* satisfy each of them. Regarding practical matters, he asked each of them to name five favorite dinner menus. "Now we have fifteen meals we can rotate and be sure that at least one person is pretty happy. There are even a few meals you boys enjoy fixing on your own." Other complaints about practical matters were handled in pretty much the same way.

It was obvious that Ricky's outbursts were not about menus or timetables but about feelings of anger he couldn't express in another way. Ricky's dad let both boys know he understood and respected their anger. "But," he told them, "that doesn't mean I'm going to be a dumping ground for it. I won't tolerate insults or cursing. When your anger gets that strong, pound a pillow, run around the track, or go down to the basement and yell and scream." It helped Ricky a lot to know he could "let it out" but not "take it out" on his dad or anyone else.

FRED

Most of us are troubled from time to time about what to do with angry feelings. When children feel anger toward someone they love, they may feel guilty about that anger, too. Both anger and guilt are difficult to deal with and parents need to take time to help children cope with them. One of our songs on *Mister Rogers' Neighborhood* is about anger:

What Do You Do?

What do you do with the mad that you feel
When you feel so mad you could bite?
When the whole wide world seems oh, so wrong
And nothing you do seems very right?
What do you do? Do you punch a bag?
Do you pound some clay or some dough?
Do you round up friends for a game of tag?
Or see how fast you go?

It's great to be able to stop
When you've planned a thing that's wrong.
And be able to do something else instead
And think this song:

I can stop when I want to,
Can stop when I wish,
Can stop, stop, stop anytime.
And what a good feeling to feel like this,
And know that the feeling is really mine
Know that there's something deep inside
That helps us become what we can,
For a girl can be someday a woman
And a boy can be someday a man.

CLARE

Ricky was able to express his anger, even if at first only indirectly, because he knew his father loved him and felt safe and secure in his belief that nothing would make his father leave. He did not have these same safe feelings about his mother. When Ricky and Don were with her, Ricky thought only of pleasing her, afraid that any "bad behavior"

might permanently drive her away. This response is not
unusual.

FRED

Almost every parent I talked with felt confused when their
children expressed a different attitude toward each parent.
It made some feel that the children blamed only one parent
for the divorce. Any parent in this situation could wonder,
"What did I do to deserve this?"

I learned from Dr. Margaret McFarland (*Mister Rogers'
Neighborhood*'s chief consultant for over two decades) that
children are most likely to express their deepest feeling to a
person with whom they feel truly safe. Sometimes that
person is neither the mother nor the father. Following a
divorce, some children feel so hurt by the loss of one
parent they imagine their anger could cause the loss of
both. In one family I know, the eleven-year-old chose a
loving aunt. For this girl, her aunt was the safest person.
She helped her niece remember to keep her anger focused
on what was actually causing it, and she helped her find
ways to be angry without hurting anyone.

Facing a child's anger and judgment can be hard, but
talking about it is one of the best ways to help that phase
pass. Something I often say is "Anything human is mentionable, and anything mentionable *can* be manageable." I
believe that's true.

SUMMARY

- Some preteens revert to childish behavior, others
  feel they have to "stand in" for the parent who left
  home.

- It is most helpful to keep the lines of responsibility clear: grown-ups take care of grown-up problems.

- Many children want to "fix" their parents' lives in order to take their sadness away.

- Some children work very hard to bring home the parent who has left. It helps when a child is told that their parents' separation is as permanent as their love and commitment to their children.

- It is not unusual for children to act stern and judgmental about a divorce. They often blame one parent or the other.

CHAPTER 6

EFFECTS OF SEPARATION ON ADOLESCENTS

CLARE

Adolescence is an emotionally turbulent state regardless of what is happening in the home. Teenagers are working hard to discover who they are as individuals, what they believe in, and what their aspirations are. It is not unusual for the same girl who, in the morning, went off to school saying, "I can't talk to you about anything—you never understand" to come home seeking advice on some life or death matter that she's sure only you can deal with.

Adolescents are apt to view things from extremes as a way of discovering attitudes about which they are comfortable. Erica told me, "I'll just *die* if my parents don't get back together. My whole life will be ruined forever." Though others will say the opposite of what they mean, the response is equally exaggerated. Alex told me, "I couldn't care less about my parents' divorce. I just want to get out of the house as soon as I can." The fact was, and he later realized, he cared so deeply he couldn't admit it to himself.

Not surprisingly, the reactions of teenagers to divorce are often the most outrageous of any age and can cause parents considerable worry. In some ways, even though they are likely to be able to understand and accept the reasons for it, adolescents have a particularly complicated experience with divorce. Teenagers are in the midst of the very important stage in the development of identity: separation from their parents and movement toward independence and emotional maturity. It takes several years for children to finish this work of adolescence. A lot of us remember these years as the most difficult and challenging of our lives. Teenagers are constantly testing the limits of support and freedom. Teenagers will take a few steps away, then come back home, a comfortable place to restore a sense of confidence and security. Once replenished, they are ready to go out again, try new things, growing a little more independent with each step. When a couple with teenagers divorce, the children feel they have lost the security of their home base, and often the process of seeking independence is arrested.

> Eileen's parents separated when she was sixteen years old. According to her mother's description of the marriage, the relationship had grown increasingly difficult over the previous five years. Yet Eileen's picture of her parents' marriage is quite different. "They were so happy," she told me, "that I can't understand why they would ever do something like this. I feel like my whole life has ended. Nothing will ever fix the emptiness I feel now."

Eileen's response is not at all unusual for a person her age. She thought her parents were happy, because they still did many of the same things together and because both parents were involved in her life in the way they always had been. "Like anyone else her age, Eileen has a lot of romantic notions," her mother told me. "Just because her father and I went out to dinner and saw the same friends, Eileen imagined we were feeling the same inside as we always had. I think her reaction is pretty typical."

Both of Eileen's parents realized how much she needed to have a feeling of home as a secure place to come back to whenever she needed it. "What my husband and I showed Eileen was that we would still be her home base, but as individuals instead of a couple," her mother said. Eileen's family was able to sort out some very important feelings about the divorce. I think one reason the family was successful is the level of understanding Eileen was able to bring to the situation. Even though it took her a long time to comprehend why her parents would even consider divorce, she was able to accept their decision and adapt to the new family structure. Generally, teenage children are able to bring some degree of maturity to adult problems, and this can be a big help at such a time.

FRED

Divorcing parents are sometimes worried by what teenagers will say during this time, statements that are actually common adolescent responses to stress. One mother talked with me about her son's idea to drop out of school at fifteen and go to New York and become an actor. He told his mother he had no family to stay at home for, that he'd rather manage on his own in New York. Naturally his mother was worried.

Most of the time these fantasies are just that—fantasies. But in the fantasy there is often a search for limits, a testing to see whether anyone still cares enough to go on acting like a parent. Since the teenage years are usually turbulent times anyway (there are so many bodily changes going on inside and out), what adolescents may want most is the reassurance from their parents that those parents *will* set limits on potentially destructive behavior and will be there when they're needed. Another common fantasy was told to me by one girl:

> "When my parents divorced, I was sixteen. I was crushed. I remember spending a lot of time lying on my bed entertaining morbid fantasies about being orphaned. Sometimes I would imagine my entire family wiped out in a car accident. The whole town came out to comfort me. Everyone felt sorry for me. I had the house to myself. All the money was mine and nobody was around to make demands on me.
>
> "Then thoughts of my mother would creep in. I'd think, well, I'd miss her too much. The accident got revised—and she was saved. As I thought about each person, I decided I didn't really want to live without any one of them. One by one I saved them. They may not be perfect, but the family was mine."

Several other teenagers shared their thoughts with me and talked about fantasies like this. Some parents never hear of them, and some learn about them years after the divorce. I can imagine that a parent hearing about a violent daydream might feel upset, but I believe such fantasies can help diffuse some of the anger and confusion that adolescents feel and can help them think through their closest relationships. Teenagers often work through many basic feelings in this kind of way.

CLARE

A number of teenagers expressed anger about divorce forcing them into independence before they were ready. The pull between the need for freedom and the need for the security of home is common to most teenagers. A divorce at this time may exaggerate normal mood swings. I think it's important for teenagers to be assured that their parents will provide as secure a home base as possible while allowing freedoms appropriate to previously established family values. This assurance of continuity is important for all teenagers but particularly so for those whose home life is undergoing the dramatic changes of divorce.

Some children have a tendency to look to outside comforts to fill some of the emptiness they feel inside. Two common comforts children talked of are food and possessions.

> James gained forty pounds in four months after his mother moved out. "I don't ever remember feeling hungry, but I always *needed* food. It was the weirdest thing," he said. "When I came home from school I would make two sandwiches, wash them down with soda, and then start on a family-sized bag of potato chips. When my father got home, I'd eat a regular dinner. By eight o'clock I was back in the kitchen again."

At first, James had a difficult time understanding what food meant to him during these months, but he became very upset by what was happening to his body. Even though he was not athletic, he had been an enthusiastic participant in school gym classes. Now he was unable to complete simple warm-up exercises. The more James ate, the more tired and depressed he felt. He spent a lot of time alone, frequently eating in front of the television set or in his room.

This inclination to withdraw into food when feeling sad or lonely was expressed again and again. As one girl told me:

"I had this big empty hole inside me after Dad left. All I wanted to do was fill up that hole. Some days I would walk home from school and have a Cherry Coke and French fries at one place, walk two more blocks and get a slice of pizza to eat on the way home. I really never thought about how I looked or even whether I was hungry. All I wanted to do was fill that awful hole."

Children may express their needs for comfort with possessions:

"When Dad moved out," John told me, "I became 'thing' crazy. 'Buy me' could have been my middle name. It's easy to get your parents to give you things when they're getting a divorce, because they feel real sorry for you."

Then John told me something that made me feel wonderful.

"After I had this pile of stuff, I realized nothing anybody *bought* me would make me feel good inside. I would have to find *that* somewhere inside myself. Even though the presents didn't make me feel better, I came to understand that my parents cared about how I felt. I knew they wanted me to feel better, because they loved me a whole lot. I thought I might lose their love with the divorce, but I didn't at all."

FRED

We all experience sad and lonely times, times when we feel a "hole" inside. And most of us have to learn that when we suffer through losing someone we love, material things such as new clothing or a record player will never make that sadness go away. Material things can, in fact, sometimes make us feel emptier. Once we see how temporary a satisfaction they bring, that disappointment can make us feel even more lonely. Many children I spoke with had learned this and felt a lot better for growing through the experience.

CLARE

A few parents talked with me about children "manipulating" them during the post-separation time. As one mother put it, "Margaret plays me against her father to get her way." Using the word "manipulation" to describe this behavior in a child who is experiencing divorce makes me uncomfortable. It suggests that the child is willfully trying to take advantage of his or her parents' difficult situation. The behavior of children might indicate that this is the case, but I don't believe that this is the intent. I think they are finding ways to test their parents' limits and the security of their environment. "Daddy lets me stay up until ten, and you make me go to bed at 8:30" may really mean "Do you love me as much as Daddy?" or "Do you love me at all after the divorce?"

FRED

During the teen years, when so much feels off-balance, children may try lots of different ways to get back on firm footing. Keeping limits clear is always helpful for children, but for teenagers it is crucial. Some of us find this difficult. One father told me the following story:

> "From the moment I laid eyes on my daughter I adored her. She's a most special child. The hardest thing about divorcing my wife was losing daily contact with my daughter. I really hurt her terribly with the divorce. She always seemed so sad and angry. Sometimes her anger seemed to get worse instead of better. She grew so demanding. I hardly recognized her anymore. Often I was tempted to give in to her demands, but I knew it wouldn't be good if I gave her everything she asked for.
>
> "One day she asked for a new tape recorder with earphones. It cost a hundred dollars. It wasn't the money, though. I just don't think it's a good idea for kids to get expensive things at the drop of a hat. When I explained that I thought the recorder could wait for her birthday, my daughter told me she hated me. Her anger really hurt!"

That father wanted to give his daughter everything she asked for, particularly after the divorce, when he was so distressed about no longer living with her. But he understood that it was more important for him to accept her anger and disappointment than to give in to her demands. "When she said she hated me," he recalled, "I told her I was very sorry she felt that way, because I loved her very much. After a few similar incidents she believed me and the demands stopped."

It takes a lot of patience for any parent to turn the other

cheek. Anger and rejection from people we love can hurt a great deal. But a teenager needs as much strong "parenting" as any child. Teenagers rely on their parents to help them find a way out of the confusion of the changes the adolescent years bring, and even during a divorce parents *can* provide the guidance their children need. The absence of one parent on a daily basis can make it all the more difficult, but the extra effort is so worthwhile!

CLARE

When a divorce occurs, some parents observe two pronounced reactions in their adolescents: strong clashes with the parent of the same sex and a closer relationship with the parent of the opposite sex.

> "When my husband and I divorced," Evelyn told me, "our son and daughter were in their teens. My daughter and I battled constantly. Though our arguments were more vehement, I was reminded of my own teenage struggles with my mother—and my parents weren't divorced. Sometimes it took more strength than I had to put up with the arguing and criticism. In the middle of our worst time I embroidered myself a pillow that said: 'If you don't have anything nice to say, come sit here beside me.' That always gave me a chuckle. If I couldn't laugh, I never would have made it through that time."

Evelyn's memory of her own high school years helped her understand how normal and necessary are the struggles between teenagers and the parent of the same sex. Even so, I'm sure that Evelyn had moments of feeling tired and frustrated.

> "My son Donald was the exact opposite of Pam," Evelyn went on. "He thought I was simply wonderful. Accord-

ing to Donald, every meal I cooked would bring Julia Child to her knees. Don's struggles were with his father. At times I found his blind acceptance of me very seductive. Not only was it a relief from Pam's constant criticism, but I secretly liked the fact that he was giving his father such a hard time.

"I knew that Donald needed me to pull away a little bit. It was important for him to see me and his father more realistically in our roles as parents, not as friend or foe. I found myself in the position of defending his father and sister, neither of whom were being particularly nice to me. It got pretty wild, but there's one thing having teenagers teaches you—and that is to expect the unexpected. Maybe I'll make that my next pillow!"

Evelyn's sense of humor and her sensitivity helped her remember that all adolescents are in an emotionally turbulent state regardless of what is happening in the home. Being around young people while they are working hard to discover who they are, what they believe in and where they will go with their lives can stir up dust that never seems to settle.

SUMMARY

- Adolescents often have pronounced, extreme reactions to a divorce, which reflect the complex pattern of their emotional development.

- Some teenagers have romantic fantasies that make understanding the reality of divorce very difficult for them.

- Generally, teenagers are able to bring some degree of maturity to adult problems. It helps to be honest with them, without burdening them with inappropriate details about the divorce.

- It helps everyone when we, as parents, try to understand which behavior patterns are cries for limit-setting.

- Some teenagers feel pushed by divorce into independence before they are ready.

- During the teen years, when so much of their lives feels off-balance, our children may act rebelliously before they can get back on firm ground.

SECTION II

LIVING
THROUGH
THE SEPARATION
AND
EVENTUAL
DIVORCE

CHAPTER 7

HELPING CHILDREN UNDERSTAND THEIR REACTIONS OF AMBIVALENCE AND RELIEF

FRED

Children I talked with described feelings of *ambivalence* about their parents' divorce: They felt two quite different ways about it. We all have ambivalent feelings. I usually feel ambivalent about travel. Sometimes I'm planning to do something so interesting that I'm glad to go, but at the same time part of me wants to stay home with my family and friends in familiar surroundings. Ambivalence is something most adults understand, but for children it can be puzzling.

I remember my son's first day of school. We all felt ambivalent that day! As we left the house, he was exhilarated by the adventure waiting for him. For months he had talked about the excitement of going to school "like the big kids," but as we got closer to the building, he reached for my hand. I knew that he was scared to be on his own in this strange, new place.

His mother and I had similar feelings that day, too. We

felt excited and proud about this big new step our son was taking, but there was some sadness as well: "Our son is growing up and we'll miss him." Of course, as adults, we could understood our ambivalence—and his; we'd known about that word for a long time. But it took our son a long while to feel comfortable with his ambivalent feelings.

Ambivalent feelings are very common in divorce. "I'm glad the fighting is finally over," one girl told me, "but I want my father back home like always." Another girl wondered, "I am glad I don't have to listen to hassles all day, but does that mean I want my parents to divorce?" Many children have a strong wish to stay together as a family but an equally strong desire to live in a home without fighting.

> "My father moved out after a couple of years of cold war," one sixteen-year-old said. "It was really pretty intense. The last few months there was a lot of fighting. Then Dad was gone. Sometimes the house was so quiet, and it felt so good. Other times the quiet made me feel sad and miss my Dad a whole lot. It was so confusing. I could never be sure of what I felt.
>
> "When I started eighth grade, we got some vocabulary study books. Each week we learned twelve new words. In the second week there was this new word: 'Ambivalence, the existence of positive and negative feelings toward the same person, object or action.' That became my million-dollar word. Our teacher had this saying, 'Use a new word in a sentence ten times and it's yours for life.' Well, I must have used ambivalence a hundred times."

Learning the word *ambivalent* helped relieve that boy of some of the conflict he felt about his parents' divorce. Knowing that it was okay to feel ambivalent was liberating for him. When children are old enough to understand about ambivalence, parents may want to talk about it with them. Big words can be intimidating, but even so, putting names to feelings can often make it easier for people to accept them.

A friend's six-year-old daughter, Ellen, had made arrangements to spend the afternoon with a neighborhood friend. In the meantime, another friend called to invite Ellen to a nearby amusement park. Ellen was clearly feeling divided about what she wanted to do: "I want so much to go to the park," she said, "but I want to play next door, too. And I don't want to hurt anyone's feelings."

I was having lunch with the family that day. Ellen's mother took her on her lap and talked with her about conflicting feelings. This mother explained that we all feel divided from time to time, that it was perfectly natural to want two desirable things at the same time. They also talked about how Ellen's friend might feel if Ellen changed plans simply because something more exciting came along. Ellen was able to put herself in her friend's place and decided to stay with the original plans. "I would feel bad if I hurt her feelings," Ellen told her mother. "Then the park wouldn't be much fun anyway."

Once young children have worked through the puzzle of ambivalence, they may worry about having happy feelings about something as sad as divorce. They also may act one way and then another, or say two conflicting things almost in the same minute. It's important for parents to accept that these seeming contradictions are true reflections of how a child feels at that moment: different ways about the same thing.

CLARE

When divorce means an end to overt family tensions or arguments, it's only natural for many children to feel relieved. Still, parents wonder if a child's relief indicates a lack of caring about the family. The relief, however, is most often an indication that the child cares a great deal.

> "The sound of the key in the front door made my stomach knot," Hannah told me. "That meant my father was home and he and my mother might start fighting again. They didn't always fight, but I never knew what to expect. I've always hated fighting."

Many children are sensitive to noise and tension. When a divorce signals the end to these circumstances, children often feel free to have a relationship with each parent without the worry of a pending explosion. "I always felt I was in the way when my parents argued," one girl told me. Anyone who has been present when an argument flares up between two other people will understand how uncomfortable this situation makes a person feel. If the two people fighting are people we love, the feelings of discomfort are likely to be magnified. Anything that helps stop the fighting can come as a welcome relief.

One father, Don, told me the following story.

> "Martha and I had some tremendous arguments before we separated. This may sound odd, but I think our fights were so intense because we really didn't want to let the marriage go. Sometimes we'd work out a peace, but the best we could ever manage was a truce. And that never lasted very long.
>
> "Our son, Jon, would disappear whenever the fighting

started. Later he told me he'd go anywhere just to get away from the sounds of our fights.

"One summer day, about a year after the divorce, Jon and I were resting under a shade tree at the park. We had been lying quietly, just trying to keep cool.

"'If I tell you a secret, do you promise you won't get mad?' Jon asked me. I couldn't imagine what Jon was about to tell me, but I assured him I wanted to hear anything he'd like to tell me.

"'When you and Mom got divorced, I felt glad. No more fights! No more hiding in my room. Does that make you mad?' Jon asked.

"This was one of those fragile moments. My son shared with me something of serious concern to him, and he was worried about how I'd react. He thought I'd be hurt or angry because of his glad feelings.

"I remembered a time when I felt the way Jon did. So I shared it with him. My father had been ill for a while, and we knew that he would die shortly. His illness caused him considerable pain. Some days, the simple movement of a bedsheet over his leg would make him cry out in pain.

"I told my son about leaving the hospital and saying a prayer, asking God to take my Dad and spare him more physical pain.

"God didn't take my Dad that night. Dad didn't close his eyes for the last time for several more days, but when he did, I felt guilty about my prayer and about my feeling of relief. Then I realized, and this is what I told Jon, that the relief I felt didn't mean that I didn't love my Dad. It simply meant that I didn't want to have to watch my Dad suffer so much pain."

It is not hard to imagine why Jon wanted to keep his relief about his parents' divorce secret; his glad feelings made him feel guilty. When someone we love is in pain, we want their hurt to end. It helped Jon to know that his father had the same kind of feelings about his own father, even though their circumstances were not the same.

SUMMARY

- When divorce brings an end to family tension, it is natural for children to have feelings of relief.

- It is important for parents to remember that when a child acts one way and then another, or says conflicting things, it is not because the child wants to be disruptive, but rather because the child actually feels different ways at different times.

- Many children will worry about having happy feelings about something as "sad" as divorce. It is up to parents to help them understand that we all sometimes feel two different ways about the same thing.

CHAPTER 8

HELPING CHILDREN UNDERSTAND THEIR SEPARATION REACTIONS OF GRIEF

CLARE

Most children feel great sadness, even depression, when parents separate, particularly if they have a close or dependent relationship to the parent who moves out. Some children become preoccupied with thoughts about the departed parent; even though that parent is not lost to them forever, they sense that the relationship will never be the same. The natural expression of grief is probably the most significant step every family member takes in the process of adjusting to a divorce. It is through grieving that people begin to be healed.

Elizabeth was ten when her mother died. As the youngest child in a large family, she was particularly close to her mother. The loss devastated her. She lived through the first months following the death without showing many feelings at all. Eventually she developed difficulties sleeping and eating. She was diligent in school but had trouble concentrating. Sometimes she would lie awake for three or four hours before she went to sleep. Her father was troubled by what was happening to her but felt helpless to understand what to do for her. He could not imagine that she, at ten, was having the same feelings as he. One night he went into her room and saw that she was awake well past midnight. As they talked about what had happened, expressions of frustration and feelings of inadequacy poured out of both of them. They embraced and cried for a long time.

Elizabeth and her father had begun to *share* the grief each had been experiencing alone. Children who have had a great loss, particularly if it is a first experience, need help living through, and expressing their grief. Giving help can be difficult for parents who are troubled by grief of their own or, as sometimes happens in divorce, so filled with anger that they cannot imagine what a child would grieve over. But the departure of a parent, through divorce or death, can be a traumatic loss to the child. Though in the case of divorce the parent is still alive, he or she will not be available to the child in the same way as before.

Sadness is a common reaction and usually passes after a time. Some people put a premium on being "brave" or "strong" when they experience a loss. Some people told me of doctors who prescribe tranquilizers for patients who lost someone close "to help the grieving person through it." But suppressing grief only prolongs its pain. Encouraging a child to "be a big boy" or "act like a grown-up" can damage his or her chance to work through grief's natural progression and invite more difficulties later.

Some parents believe they can talk their children out of sad feelings. And that's what they try to do. I think that's because it hurts to see our children sad for any reason. "My parents were always telling me not to be sad," a sixteen-year-old boy told me. " 'Lots of kids are far worse off than you,' they'd tell me. That's like telling someone who lost his house in a hurricane that he was lucky to have a house to lose."

Ricky was five when his parents separated and for a while, he felt terribly sad. During the first few weeks he was tearful. The kindergarten teachers told his mother that Ricky never got through a day when something didn't bring him to tears. But they felt sure Ricky would return to "his old self" once he adjusted to his parents' separation.

"The thought of such a young boy burdened by such sadness broke my heart," she told us. "Without really thinking about what I was doing, I started reminding Ricky of his father's faults. I guess I thought that if Ricky didn't think his father was so great, maybe he'd stop missing him."

What Ricky's mother did only made Ricky's loss seem greater. It would have helped Ricky if his mother had encouraged him to talk about *his* feelings openly.

FRED

Even if a child's life is full with friends and school and activities, parents remain the center of a child's life. Many children told me, "I want Mommy—*but I want Daddy too.*"

One seven-year-old talked about the sad feelings he had for a while after his parents' divorce. "When I'm with my Dad, I really miss Mom," he told me. "When Mom takes me for a visit, then I think about Dad and miss him." That boy's words made me remember a magazine cover I saw a few years ago. The feature article was about divorce, and the cover showed a snapshot of a mother and father holding the hands of a young child. The photograph was torn right down the middle of the child. That's probably just how that seven-year-old was feeling—torn between two parents he loved. For a while he wasn't able to enjoy fully the time he spent with either parent. But each parent continued to talk with him and after a time, he was more comfortable with his feelings.

Deep sadness is a normal and healthy response to a loss. Children should be able to feel sad, or to cry, for as long as they need to. Even when a child recovers from the sadness, it is common that a thought or memory will once again bring sudden tears. One man whose parents divorced twenty-five years ago expressed it this way: "The sadness goes away. Then at some unexpected time, in some ordinary place, it hits you and you cry a little. It's never completely gone. I'm not so sure it should be."

If I could wish one thing for divorcing parents, it would be that they find the strength and understanding to keep their feeling toward one another separate from their children's feeling toward *them*. A divorce is between husband and wife, not between parent and child. It does not help children grieve when parents add marital anger to their children's sadness.

SUMMARY

- When parents separate, most children feel great sadness, or even depression. This natural expression of grief is probably the most significant step every family member takes in the process of adjusting to a divorce and it is important that these expressions are shared.

- Parents should encourage their children to talk about their feelings.

- Parents need to try to keep their feelings toward one another separate from their children's feelings toward them.

CHAPTER 9

HELPING CHILDREN UNDERSTAND THEIR REACTIONS OF ANGER

CLARE

During separation and divorce, everyone has some anger to manage. All of us experience anger when our wishes and hopes are disrupted—it is quite natural to react this way—and it is extremely important that we learn constructive ways to express that anger. Children might cry, misbehave, throw tantrums, become sullen, or even strive for unreasonable perfection, but whatever the outward signs, they especially need their parents help to understand this powerful emotion. Respect and acceptance of all feelings help children grow into people who respect themselves as well as others.

Expressions of anger should not be allowed to hurt another person or thing. One of our most important parental responsibilities is helping our children understand some important limits—limits they will need to observe their whole life long. Some limits are important for our safety; others help us live comfortably in a world we share with others. Understanding what these limits on anger are makes children feel more comfortable as they find their way in the world.

FRED

Anger can be very frightening to children. When an adult is angry, a child might worry that he or she has lost the love of that person. When it is the child who is angry, the feeling of losing control can be equally scary: Children may imagine that they might actually hurt people they love, and, once again, lose the love of those persons.

There have been times when I've watched a two-year-old in a tantrum and thought, "I was that angry just this morning." No life is free from frustrations. It can help children to know that we adults get angry, too, particularly when we mention some of the constructive ways we have found to let our anger out. Knowing that everyone has to strive for control over anger can help children go on striving for the inner control they need—*and want.*

CLARE

Throughout the times of separation and divorce, each family member is struggling with their own unique feelings of anger. It's very hard to address someone else's anger when we are feeling angry ourselves.

Our children's anger can take the often perplexing form, particularly if they have not learned to understand such complicated feelings of seemingly deliberate misbehavior.

All children misbehave from time to time, and through the distress of divorce, they may misbehave more often.

Some parents told me about aggressiveness among brothers and sisters or with friends. Others talked about foul language. Some of these problems are simply the way a particular child reacts to stress. Usually they are worked out quite well with parents and teachers.

What is even more important than changing the behavior is understanding and talking about the feelings.

Alexandra was five when her parents separated. A bright, active child, she had experienced some minor, normal difficulties staying focused on school activities. After her father moved out of their home, Alexandra's teachers noticed a sharp increase in her problems at school. Her tendency toward distraction became exaggerated to the point that she frequently interrupted lessons, annoying the teacher and her classmates. Always forthright and spontaneous, she began to talk out in class and argue with her classmates. Alexandra's parents became concerned about the frequent reports from school and felt sure that their separation was to blame.

It is not unusual for parents to feel that *all* misbehavior and all of the anger in their children is directly related to the problems in their marriage or their divorce, although this could not ever be true. Alexandra's way of behaving existed before the separation. What were minor difficulties before the separation became exaggerated during a time of *her* greatest stress, but were not entirely out of character. Fortunately, her teacher was sympathetic and was able to help Alexandra and her parents understand some important things. In school the teacher made clear that she expected Alexandra to follow the established routines and respect the rights of all her classmates. Eventually, and it took nearly the entire school year, Alexandra was able to control her anger and concentrate on her activities most of the time; she was more attentive, her paperwork was neater, and her relationship to her classmates greatly improved. She was not "perfect"; a reaction that would have been just as indicative of stress as the previous misbehavior. Her behavior was appropriate for her age, and that was all that her understanding teacher had expected.

Sometimes, a child will have a particularly angry or violent outburst. This can be very frightening.

> One older boy I talked with, Mark, recalled an evening when he was about seven. He went to dinner at a classmate's house because his father, with whom he lived after his parents divorced, had an unexpected emergency at work that required him to stay late. During dinner he sat quietly with his friend Katherine and her family while they talked about the day at school. In the middle of the meal, Mark suddenly jumped up, ran to Katherine's room and started throwing her toys and books around.

Mark's behavior was a reflection of the fury he felt about the unexpected change in his father's plans. But his anger was also a holdover of feelings engendered by his parents' separation and divorce. Many children I talked with said it was the angry feelings that caused them the greatest difficulty. "For a long time I felt very, very sad," an eight-year-old girl told me. "When the sad feelings went away, I was angry all the time." It is essential for parents to help their children learn that there are ways to be angry that don't hurt people or their possessions.

With Mark, Katherine's parents were quick to address his angry feelings. First, they put a stop to the outburst. Katherine's mother said, "No matter how angry you feel, I cannot let you do this to Katherine's room." Sensing that he was still quite upset, Katherine's mother held Mark until he was calmer. Once Mark was quiet, Katherine's dad told him, "I understand how upset you are. When your dad had to change plans for the evening, it made you very, very angry. A surprise like that could make me angry, too." Everyone helped Mark restore order to Katherine's room. Mark learned a great deal from this experience. First, and most important, was that angry *feelings* are okay but cannot be expressed in ways that hurt anyone. He also learned that feeling "let down" can make anyone angry, even grown-ups. When everyone helped Mark straighten the mess, he may also have learned that he could ask for and accept help in "straightening out the mess" he felt his own life to be.

FRED

Some parents talked to me about how helpful friends were during the period following their separation and divorce. Caring adults who are not directly involved in the conflicts of a divorce can be particularly helpful to children during this time. They can listen without making judgments, they can help children understand their different feelings, and they may be able to talk with them about some of the things divorcing families feel.

CLARE

Mark's father learned a lot after hearing about the events at Katherine's house, particularly because they were told to him in a way that made him understand his son's feelings.

Divorcing parents frequently need help in seeing through their own pain and anger.

> Kendra's twin boys were six when she divorced. Her most vivid memory of the period following the separation was the boys' seemingly endless scrapping. At home

they fought with each other; at the playground they fought with their friends. It seemed that no one invited the boys to play anymore. Kendra eventually resorted to harsh spankings as punishment, a form of discipline she had never used and one that filled her with guilt and remorse.

Unfortunately, divorcing parents are faced with the double challenge of managing their own rage and that of their children. All parents I talked with describe this as the most difficult task. They are called upon to perform parental tasks that are difficult, under normal circumstances, at a time when their inner resources are exhausted. A father put it this way: "I feel like I have practically no energy left after working all day. When the kids start up, all I have the strength to do is spank them and send them to their rooms."

FRED

One working mother of four told me that she arrived home each evening feeling tired and in need of a few minutes of relaxation before preparing dinner and completing other household chores. Instead of finding a small pocket of quiet, she found arguments and a four-way competition for her attention. Out of her frustration she came up with a plan that other parents have found useful: Each time an argument got out of control, she signaled a "time-out." When that signal was made, each person had to find a place and cool down for ten minutes. When the cooling-off period ended, the children were usually able to settle their differences. To help herself, she developed a ritual of coming home, greeting the children and going straight into a hot shower for relaxation. That seemed to give the children time to adjust to her return as well, and often they forgot their differences and could talk about some of the things that bothered them and were making them angry, or about things that made them happy.

Parents who can remind themselves that anger is a normal and acceptable reaction to divorce are likely to have an easier time accepting anger in themselves and their children. Children's anger can come out in lots of different ways, many of which may really be bids for attention from the parents they fear they are losing. One mother told us she returned from work one day to see her four-year-old daughter painted from shoulder to forehead in permanent colored markers. Her face and parts of her hair were covered in brilliant hues that stayed on her skin for several days. The babysitter told this mother that when she discovered what the child had done, she asked, "What on earth will your mother say?" The child, looking in the mirror, answered, "She'll look at me and say, 'Why, Mary, you look like a beautiful clown.'"

Naturally, that wasn't her mother's reaction, but aware that her daughter had been testing limits in nursery school as well, she could see a pattern in her daughter's behavior. "When I saw that face covered in colors, I wanted to scream," her mother told me. "It took tremendous control simply to tell her to use her markers on drawing paper. Then we took out some paper and drew pictures of clowns until suppertime."

That story reminds me of one of our songs on *Mister Rogers' Neighborhood:*

The Clown in Me

A clown, a clown.
I think I'll be a clown.
I think I'll make the people laugh
    and laugh all over town.
A clown, that's what I'll be . . . a clown.

Sometimes I feel, when I'm afraid,
That I will never make the grade.
So I pretend I'm someone else
    and show the world my other self.
I'm not quite sure of me, you see,
When I have to make a clown of me.

A clown, a clown.
I think I'll be a clown.
I think I'll make the people laugh
    and laugh all over town.
A clown, that's what I'll be . . . a clown.

Sometimes I feel all good inside
And haven't got a thing to hide.
My friends all tell me I'm the best;
They think I'm better than the rest.
It's times like this I act myself
And let the clown stay on the shelf.

Myself, Myself
I think I'll be myself.
I think I'll let the people see
    the comfortable inside of me.
Myself . . . I'll be myself.

It's only when I feel let down
I might be scared into a clown
But he can be himself
When I can be . . .
Myself, Myself
I think I'll be myself.

I think Mary must have been feeling unsure, as all children do from time to time, and, of course, living through their parents' separation can often cause children to feel unsure of a lot of things!

CLARE

An angry older child may seek attention from parents by insulting them or belittling something about the way they live. Malcolm liked to tell his father that his father's friends were superficial and shallow. "I got so tired of hearing his insults, I simply wanted to shut him up. Somehow, without rancor, I managed to tell Mal that he was entitled to his opinions and that when the time came, he would be able to choose his own way to live. But I also made it clear that his insults hurt my feelings and that I didn't want to be the target of his abuse. I think he was somewhat surprised and pleased that his opinions really made a difference to me."

Eric insisted from the very beginning that he was not angry about his parents' divorce. At thirteen, he was sure he was too old for such a babyish feeling. True to his word, he never expressed an angry thought.

For a long time, Eric's act fooled everyone. But what he kept from himself, did show up in his actions: He would "forget" to call his mother when he knew he'd be late; his father's birthday passed without any mention of it. The anger he felt toward both parents was evident in his seemingly total disregard for their feelings.

One day Eric's father told him that Eric's actions had hurt his father's feelings. That remark triggered a burst of anger from Eric.

Eric's parents talked with their son and helped him understand that people of every age feel anger. There is nothing babyish about any of our feelings. It's what we *do* with them that shows growth.

Many children said that fear kept them from sharing their feelings of anger with their parents. As one girl told us, "I was sure if my mother knew how angry I was, she'd leave too. After all, my father left because of all the fights."

Parents should be particularly alert to attention-getting measures that have serious consequences, such as stealing, truancy, drugs or food disorders. They require firm and prompt intervention. Parents who do not feel up to handling this situation alone can ask for help. School counselors usually have a great deal of experience with such situations. A parent who in working through difficulties uses all the resources he or she can find provides the best possible model for the children. When children see that parents aren't afraid to ask for help, they may not be so reluctant to seek help when they feel they need it.

SUMMARY

- Because children often cannot understand the complicated feelings of anger, their anger often comes out in forms of misbehavior.

- All children need to learn that there are ways to express their anger that don't hurt people or harm their possessions.

- Parents who remember that anger is a normal and acceptable reaction to divorce will have an easier time accepting these feelings in themselves and in their children.

CHAPTER 10

HELPING CHILDREN UNDERSTAND THEIR REACTIONS OF DENIAL AND FANTASY

FRED

Young children often express their "inner dramas" through fantasy. Finding words for important feelings can be hard; playing about them comes more naturally. We devote some portion of every *Mister Rogers' Neighborhood* program to visiting a place we call the Neighborhood of Make-Believe. There, puppets and people act out fantasy stories about experiences that may be puzzling, difficult or even frightening to think about. I like to think of the Neighborhood of Make-Believe as a safe place to try out feelings we're not quite sure about in real life.

A child's fantasy play may be as simple as pretending to be someone else or as elaborate as putting several characters into a complex situation. This sort of play can be a great help to children and to their parents: Children get to work on some deep feelings, while parents may learn about some of their children's concerns. Communication between parents and their children can grow through fantasy play.

Some children find the pain of divorce so great that they use fantasy not simply to express their emotions, but to protect themselves from too much hurt. In their own ways and through their own stories, children can begin to face just as much as they feel able to, coping with a large problem little by little. Though each child's fantasy is unique, some patterns are widely shared.

For younger children, an imaginary friend or doll or stuffed animal may become "the bad boy who sent Daddy away" or "the naughty girl who made Mommy angry."

> Gregory had a collection of stuffed toys and dolls he called "Sonnies." Some were child Sonnies and others adult Sonnies. They were the continuing characters in a drama he played out to help himself manage the feelings of rejection and anger he had when his parents divorced. Each night before bed he would turn his "bad Sonnies" —the adult ones—to the wall for punishment. The child Sonnies always behaved well and were deserving of the most favorable place on the shelf.

In this fantasy play, Gregory was dealing with his feelings of anger at his parents for the divorce. Parents who recognize these themes in their child's fantasies may be able to gently encourage their child to talk about the feelings directly.

> It was several weeks before Gregory's mother sensed the full theme of the evening ritual. One night as she was tucking her son into bed, she talked to him a little bit about his Sonnies. "At first he really didn't want to talk much about it," she told me. "I was hurt, but I realized these were his private thoughts. Just as I have things I'd rather not share with another person, so did Greg. So I left it alone.
>
> "Night after night Greg would select the 'bad grown-

up Sonnies' and turn them toward the wall. One evening after this routine, Greg clapped his hands together and said, 'Well, I guess that takes care of them. They'll learn not to leave their little boy and get a mean old divorce.'

"At last it was clear. I always knew Greg was angry about our divorce," his mother told me. "And now I knew that his evening play was a safe way he had picked to let go of some of his anger."

Greg's mother decided to address the subject directly. "I guess the little Sonnies are feeling very angry about the grown-ups' divorce," she said to Greg.

"Very mad and very, very sad," Greg answered.

"Don't you think the big Sonnies feel sad, too?" his mother asked.

"No, I don't know." And then Greg answered, "Well, I guess so."

"Divorce makes everyone feel sad and angry some of the time," Greg's mother told him. "It seems that's how divorce is for everyone."

After she kissed Greg good-night, he gave her an extra hug and kiss. Now, she says, the big Sonnies get turned to the wall much less often.

When a child resists talking about feelings openly, it may mean he or she needs to rehearse them in fantasy a while longer. It is not unusual, either, for a fantasy to fade only to reappear some time later. While parents can try to encourage direct talk about feelings, it's not something that can be forced. For a child, it takes a certain inner readiness.

CLARE

The use of fantasy is most common in younger children, but parents should not be surprised to see some evidence of it in older children as well.

Beverly's son Andy was nine when she and her husband divorced. She was totally unprepared for the return of "Binky," Andy's imaginary playmate and constant companion when he was four. Then, Binky had been a devilish little boy. He made messes in the playroom, hid peas in his napkin and always ate cookies before breakfast. The "new" Binky was the image of perfection. He completed his homework neatly and on schedule; he earned straight A's; he cleared the table without being asked; he even shampooed his hair twice a week. Significantly, Binky's parents lived happily together and "never had a fight."

"When Binky reappeared on the scene, I thought Andy was teasing me," Beverly said. "But the stories persisted, and I realized he wasn't playing games with me. I dug out my Dr. Spock only to have my worst fears confirmed: This was the behavior of a four-year-old!

"After a while I began to see a theme in Binky's story. He was always doing the things I had to keep after Andy about. Of course," Beverly continued, "the key point was that, because Binky behaved so well, his parents loved each other and never had a fight. The whole thing seemed so obvious to me, I couldn't believe I had missed it for so long."

This mother gradually, and in ways understandable to a nine-year-old, talked to her child about the reasons she and her husband separated, making it very clear that the problems leading up to the divorce were between the grown-ups and that though the situation affected him, he was in no way a cause. She let him know that he was the wonderful part of their marriage that both parents felt happy about. In time, Binky went away again.

To a child the notion of divorce is confounding; why would a person leave a home and the people who love him? As one six-year-old saw it, "If my mother didn't like all the fighting, why didn't she just stop?" Older children may find it equally puzzling. Fifteen-year-old Daniel said, "If my father didn't have to play cards every other night and my mother could learn to get off his back, we would still be a normal family."

Whether we tell our children our reasons for divorce or not, they may still make up some of their own fantasies to suit their needs. By paying close attention to the feeling expressed through these fantasies—and encouraging discussion—parents can help greatly in easing their children's fears.

> Krissy was eleven when her parents divorced. At the time, television shows and movies were filled with horror stories about people possessed by demons. "I got this idea that my mother must be 'possessed' or something. Looking back, this seems crazy, but I really believed it to be true, the reasoning being, who else but a devil could make my mother leave home?

FRED

Parents can unwittingly contribute to children's fantasies by not telling them the truth. It may be because the truth is painful, or because a parent feels guilty. There are many reasons why telling the truth can be hard, but I believe children can be trusted with the truths that concern them. These truths usually surface sooner or later, and children can in fact be spared pain if someone they love tells them the truth from the beginning.

There's one song on *Mister Rogers' Neighborhood* that is special for me. I call it "The Truth Will Make Me Free," and these are the words:

> What if I were very, very sad
> And all I did was smile?
> I wonder after a while
> What might become of my sadness?
>
> What if I were very, very angry
> And all I did was sit
> And never think about it?
> What might become of my anger?
>
> Where would they go, and what would they do,
> If I couldn't let them out?
> Maybe I'd fall, maybe get sick
> Or doubt.
>
> But what if I could know the truth
> And say just how I feel?
> I think I'd learn a lot that's real
> About freedom.
>
> I'm learning to sing a sad song when I'm sad.
> I'm learning to say I'm angry when I'm very mad.
> I'm learning to shout, I'm getting it out!
> I'm happy, learning exactly how I feel inside of me.
> I'm learning to know the truth.
> I'm learning to tell the truth.
> Discovering truth will make me free.

We've received many letters from parents who have told us how much that song has helped them *and* their children.

CLARE

Sometimes a child's fantasy can cause parents to become concerned, especially if that fantasy interferes with accepting the reality of a divorce. A child might pretend that the divorce just isn't happening, or "forget" what their parents told them about the separation. "My son pretends this isn't really happening," one mother told me. "His father hasn't lived at home for three months, and he still asks what time his father will be home for dinner." Denial, in its milder forms, is an everyday defense, used in the face of real or imagined danger. When we send our children off to school, we "deny" or "forget" the possibility that harm could come to them, even though that chance always exists. When worrying is only counterproductive, denial sometimes helps us keep focused on positive experiences.

Denial is sometimes useful for children, too, particularly very young children. A child of four who is told not to eat a cookie before dinner is certainly old enough to understand the reasons why he may not have one. But the child will sometimes "forget" and eat one anyway. Many parents are confused and frustrated by this behavior and interpret the "I forgot" as deliberate disobedience or lying. Rarely is this a fib, however. The forgetting is real. The force of the desire to have the cookie is so great that it overwhelms what the parent has told him about dinner, and so he "forgets." The child has simply put the unpleasant thought, "I can't have what I want," out of mind.

Denial is particularly helpful to children in stressful situations.

Alfred was nine and his sister four when their parents decided to separate. Their parents were especially concerned about Alfred's reaction because of his close relationship with his father, who was the departing parent. As both parents talked about their plans, everyone cried but Alfred, who said simply, "Are you done? I want to go out and play."

At first Alfred's parents thought he really did not care about the divorce. How foolish, they thought, to imagine that this close relationship was so meaningful to Alfred when he had evidently outgrown it. For some time after the separation Alfred remained stoic. In fact, he showed no outward evidence at all of being upset.

One day when Alfred's friend came to play, his mother overheard the friend ask Alfred where his father was. "On a trip," answered Alfred, "far away. In Africa, I think."

Alfred's reaction to his parents' news is not unusual. Frequently parents mistake a child's calm reaction as acceptance or resignation. Divorce is a wrenching experience for everyone. No one in the family is likely to accept it with equanimity. For some children, the stress of losing a parent is so great they deny the reality as one way to avoid the pain.

FRED

One parent told me something her son said on the day she married her second husband, Sidney. Sidney had no children and had developed a warm relationship with her son, but despite that and the fact that she'd been divorced for six years, her ten-year-old stated, "When Sidney dies, then you and Daddy can get married again."

Whether a child's denial takes the form of a private wish or a misunderstanding of fact, it's important to reaffirm what is true. It's not helpful to support children's fantasies that the divorce is not happening or that the marriage will be reconciled. One thing children need to hear again and again as they learn what's true is that they were in no way responsible for the divorce. They did nothing to cause it, and they can't fix it either. It seems that this one point cannot be emphasized too often. The notion that they were somehow responsible comes up again and again in children's conversations about their parents' divorces.

Parents who try to be open with their children about the facts of divorce usually find their children's denials less firm and less prolonged. Children are more likely to accept their feelings when their parents can do the same.

SUMMARY

- Parents should try to see their children's fantasies as helpful ways children unconsciously devise to handle the pain of divorce.

- Parents should tell their children, within the limits of their ability to understand, the real reasons for the divorce. This can spare them the need to invent reasons of their own.

- Parents who recognize certain themes in their child's fantasies should try to bring them out into the open so the child can talk about the feelings directly.

- The more open and honest parents are, the less need the child will have to deny the reality of the divorce.

CHAPTER 11

HELPING CHILDREN UNDERSTAND THEIR REACTIONS OF ANXIETY

CLARE

Divorce creates an atmosphere of such uncertainty that most children respond by showing some signs of excessive nervousness or anxiety. Things that never caused worry before can, subsequent to a divorce or separation, become matters of great concern to children.

Sarah was a child who had approached new experiences with enthusiasm. She loved school, enjoyed the company of her friends, and adapted quickly to new situations. During the period following her parents' separation, however, Sarah developed several habits that deeply troubled both her parents. It seemed to them that she now worried about everything. When she was with her mother, she expressed constant worry about her father's well-being. "Is he safe? Who is taking care of him?" Sometimes she needed to call his house four times a night just to feel reassured.

When she was with her father, she expressed similar

concern about her mother. At first both parents indulged Sarah's need to make contact with the other parent, but they found it more and more tedious as time went on.

Sarah's teacher reported that she was refusing to attend gym classes at school, making the excuse that she was afraid she'd get hurt. The teacher noted also that Sarah seemed overly concerned about many things, —the bus would make her late for music, the babysitter would not be at home when she returned from school, the new science teacher wouldn't like her. Sarah's list of worries seemed endless.

Normally Sarah and her classmates would play at one another's homes after school, but now Sarah refused to go to any house but her own.

FRED

After a divorce, children are likely to go through a period of wondering how the disrupted family will survive. They may not talk about their worries with anyone, but they're almost sure to be worried nonetheless. These concerns tend to be basic ones: "Who will feed Daddy and cook his meals? What will he do without us?" Or: "Mommy doesn't earn any money. How will we eat? Suppose someone comes into our house and tries to hurt Mommy? Who will protect her?"

Television can add to children's fears. Many children talked about "bad guys" robbing and killing, about kidnapping, and other threats of which they had no direct experience. It can be easy for parents to pooh-pooh these worries, to call them "silly," but the fact is that these worries are *real*. Taking them seriously and talking about them is a very important way to help children manage them. Whenever a child is seriously worried about something, we need to listen. By showing children we understand and respect their feelings, we can encourage them to go on sharing their concerns—whatever they may be.

CLARE

Sarah's parents, who allowed her to make three or four telephone calls to the absent parent, were surprised to learn that so many calls actually made their daughter more upset. The first call, they came to understand, allowed Sarah to see that her parent was home and safe. But allowing the successive calls only confirmed Sarah's belief that she indeed had something to worry about—"If they let me call so much, they must be worried too." Once her parents realized Sarah's reasoning, they allowed her one call to say hello. Both parents were open about what their plans were and where they would be when they were away from Sarah. The custodial parent could say, "Mommy's probably gardening or seeing a movie." Sarah's fears diminished in time and she regained her sense of confidence.

As a matter of course, some children worry more than others. It's not known precisely why this is so, but experiences shared by parents, teachers, and therapists have shown us that some children "worry" from the time they are quite young. Some people say it's because of the inborn temperament of a particular child or because it's encouraged by a nervous parent. Whatever the reason, if a child is inclined to worry or be nervous, he or she is likely to be even more so during a divorce. A woman I met recently told me the following story:

> "I was nine when my parents divorced," Meredith began. "My father was an alcoholic, so as far as the four children were concerned, having him leave the house was something of a relief. But even though my mother wanted my father and his drinking problems out of the house, the actual separation made her fall apart. Divorce, in those days, was a disgrace. She would take to

her room, sometimes for days, and the care of the four children was left to servants.

"I had always been a nervous little girl, but seeing my mother—actually, not seeing her—made me even more upset. I couldn't eat; I had stomachaches all the time. I was afraid of everything. In school I earned straight A's but approached each day as though I was not prepared for anything. I was a real mess. My family doctor suggested I see a psychiatrist. My mother found a doctor and had Greta, the maid, take me to see him. Greta assumed this as another duty, but she grumbled all the way, voicing her association of psychiatrists with asylums for insane people.

"Well, I don't have to tell you that a nervous girl, believing she was on her way to a place for the insane, whatever that meant, was not about to be reassured by the experience. I sat in the doctor's office and felt my insides turn into knots. I was terrified and completely unable to talk. Eventually everyone gave up on this approach considering it a total failure. I, of course, believed it was *my* failure.

"Though the anxiety level is much lower, I'm still a nervous adult—a nervous wife and mother. I'd always hated the feelings of worry and fear so in my late twenties, I did see a psychiatrist who was able to help me understand the source of some of my concerns. Now I am better at separating real worries from exaggerated ones, but it was my children who unlocked the most important door to my own childhood.

"I have a daughter and a son, born three years apart. From infancy my daughter was fretful; bright as can be, but slow to make adjustments to almost everything. She fussed a lot, was afraid of strangers, and new situations terrified her. The first time I took her to a sandbox, she looked at me as though I was suggesting torture. Her first pair of shoes and her first haircut are duly noted in her baby book as traumas—for her, for the shoe salesman and the barber.

"My son, on the other hand, seemed to adapt easily to everything. He ate well, napped, and always had a smile for the neighbors. He reacted to things the opposite of his sister. I was well into my thirties before I realized that, as a child, I probably had a temperament much like my own daughter and that my parents' divorce and how it was handled only intensified feelings that were already there."

Meredith learned what many parents cannot see: children are individuals and will react to situations—any situation, no matter how seemingly important or trivial—in very different ways. Divorcing parents can help their children by looking at each child's reaction in the context of his or her personality. Even though we may find some behavior irritating or difficult to handle, the way a particular child reacts is telegraphing an important message: "This is how *I* feel; please help me with *my* feelings."

Meredith was a grown woman before she understood what happened to her at the age of thirteen. "Now," she says, "I've been able to apply what I learned about myself to my own children. I can be happy for my son who feels so open to new experiences, and I can understand and respect my daughter's feelings as well. They are two unique individuals."

FRED

Many parents wonder how long it should take a child to adjust to a divorce. Just as children's reactions differ, so does the time to adjust. Adults whose parents divorced when they were young told us the full adjustment took place in small pieces throughout their lives. As one man put it, "First, there was the separation. That was the big one. But my graduation from school, my own marriage, having children—these events all revived feelings about my parents' divorce. I think it's fair to say you never *fully* recover, just as a part of you never stops feeling sad about a parent who dies."

SUMMARY

- Divorce creates an atmosphere of overwhelming uncertainty, to which a child will often respond with nervousness and anxiety.

- Parents need to understand that their children's concerns, whether about basic needs or fears about things with which they have no direct experience, are real. Taking these worries seriously and talking about them is a very important way to help children manage them.

- Children will respond to a divorce according to their own individual temperaments and will adjust to change according to their own timetables.

CHAPTER 12

HELPING CHILDREN UNDERSTAND THEIR REACTIONS OF GUILT

FRED

Shortly after we broadcast a series of programs focused on divorce, we received a letter from a pediatric nurse. She and her husband are both from divorced families. "Somewhere inside ourselves," she wrote, "are scars that will never quite heal. As a nurse, I see children whose illnesses are trigger points for a divorce, and it reminds me of the terrible feelings of guilt I experienced over the divorce of my own parents."

Assuming responsibility for the divorce, and feeling guilty about it, are very common childhood reactions. Children can imagine every little disruptive thing they've ever done—from crying too long when they were babies to spilling milk at the dinner table—to be causes for a parent to leave. One friend of ours who was six when his parents separated, had these recollections:

"To me, my parents seemed as happy as everybody else's parents. For the longest time their divorce stayed a dark mystery. Just before I'd go to sleep at night, I'd remember different things I did that made them angry: One night I let the cat out, and she didn't come back until the next day; when I was in first grade, I kept losing my mittens and hats; I teased my sister a lot. All those things made them upset with me.

"For a long time I believed I was the reason my parents broke up. I felt awful. But I never talked about it with anyone. I guess I didn't want anyone to say for sure, 'Yes, you're the reason.'

"Mom and Dad were both able to talk about the divorce. One of the things they eventually told me was that the problems were with them, not with my sister or me. In the beginning I still believed it must have been my fault. But when both of them kept telling us they loved *us*, it finally sunk in, and I felt a lot better.

"Now I'm older and I understand that kids don't make parents get a divorce, and they can't make parents stay together. But a little kid can't know that. I'm glad my parents understood."

CLARE

In children younger than six, guilt feelings are usually something of which they are not aware and about which they are unable to talk. Hidden or otherwise, every child does seem to have some feelings of guilt, feelings which are sometimes carried into their adult lives.

Joan was five when her mother and dad gave birth to identical twin boys. When the boys were four months old, her father left. "There was no fight, no drama —nothing. One day he was here, then he was gone," she said. "We were living in South Florida at the time. One unbelievably hot day, my mother packed the three of us into this wreck of a car, and we drove to Arizona to live with my aunt. We drove for five days, but in my memory, the trip took months. Everything went wrong. First one baby would cry, then the other. The car overheated; it was a mess. I wasn't sure what was happening, but remember being acutely aware that I had to be a good girl.

"We lived with my aunt until my mother got work. After ten years in Arizona, Mother moved East for a better job. No one ever mentioned my father and we never asked. I know that sounds incredible, but somehow the three of us children got the message that talk about our father was forbidden.

"When I was twenty-three years old, I got a letter from a woman who was my father's *fourth* wife. She told me that my father had died from a heart ailment. She was writing to all of his children. He had seven children by three wives, I learned.

"For days I walked around in a cloud of misery. When I was finally able to sort out all my feelings, I knew that the principal one was guilt. I realized that I had always believed my father left because *I* was not a good girl; that it was because of me that my mother's and brothers' lives were disrupted."

With this realization, Joan began a search for the truth about her father, which began with her mother. Joan's mother was reluctant to talk about the man. "He had trouble with responsibility," was all she would say. "You kids would only have been hurt by the truth."

The next stop was Joan's aunt in Arizona. Her aunt talked about the family's years in Arizona and how she believed Joan helped lighten her mother's burdens. "You were such a good little girl." From her aunt, Joan learned that her father had a history of marrying, having children, and leaving when the responsibilities got too great. "Why didn't anyone tell me any of this?" Joan asked. "There was enough hurt in your lives without talking about it," was her aunt's answer.

Joan returned home feeling terribly angry. She was furious with her aunt, her mother, *and* her father. "I found myself talking out loud to them when I was alone, having the arguments I wouldn't dare have face-to-face," she said. These feelings dominated Joan's life for another year before she took the step of visiting the woman who had been married to her father at the time of his death. This woman was quite open with Joan. She talked of a man to whom she was married for ten years, a man with four children, stepbrothers and stepsisters Joan never knew existed. When Joan was about to leave, the woman told her, "I don't know why he did the things he did, but you should know that he loved you very much; he was always talking about his little Joanie."

"After that visit, I went home and cried," Joan said. "I couldn't help but wonder why, if he loved me so much, he never tried to call me? I realized also that this was something I would never know."

It took Joan years to piece together a story that might have been explained by her mother in a way she could understand when she was five years old. In the absence of truth, Joan created her own story about the divorce and cast herself as the villain. "I always believed I caused the divorce," Joan told me, "and even though she never said so, I believed my mother blamed me for the hardship she endured putting a life together for us."

Joan's story is unusual, but her feelings are not. When parents divorce, many children feel responsible in some way, even though they may never talk about these feelings. As an adult, Joan had to search for her feelings before she could understand them. Until that happened, she told me, she focused all her energies on being "a good girl." She feels she missed a lot from her young life because of the energies spent on being "good enough."

FRED

As parents, we need to remember that when children have unanswered questions, or unspoken ones, they will invent their own answers. Often these answers are far more damaging than the harshest truth.

A few divorcing parents told me of children who refused to see one parent. There are many reasons a child might reject one parent, but fantasies and guilt often play a significant part.

> One little girl of divorced parents overheard her grandmother and mother discussing the fact that her parents had "had to get married." Even though she was too young to understand the specific meaning of the words, she was quick to infer that she was the reason for her parents' unhappiness.
>
> Thereafter she refused to spend any time with her father. At first, everyone assumed she just didn't like him anymore, but in fact she adored her father. It was her belief that she was responsible for her parents' unhappiness that were making visits with him too painful. She blamed herself, and she was sure her father blamed her too.
>
> The full truth about her feelings did not surface for several months. In school she drew a picture of a family and told her teacher a story about a girl who made everyone so unhappy that Daddy had to run away. "That's what I did," she told the teacher. "I made Mommy and Daddy so unhappy he had to go away."

Fortunately her teacher was sensitive and perceptive and called both parents to let them know what was happening. In time they were able to reassure their daughter that she had *nothing* to do with their divorce.

CLARE

In a divorce where the tension is high and the arguments frequent, parents may also argue about their children. Children who overhear these arguments—and they often do—may conclude that they caused the divorce.

> Alan had always been a quiet child who, though he played well enough with other children, frequently chose private play over group activities. His mother often took Alan to the park or arranged play dates to encourage the boy to be more outgoing; nonetheless, he remained more interested in solitary play.
>
> When Alan attended nursery school, his teachers noted this tendency at a parent conference but indicated that they believed it to be a reflection of temperament and personality, not a problem, because all other adjustments seemed healthy.
>
> While his mother was comfortable about this quality, Alan's father was very upset by it. He believed Alan was "made this way by an overprotective mother who would rather have a pansy than a real boy." When trouble between the couple intensified, arguments about Alan became more frequent. After they divorced, nothing could convince Alan that he was not to blame. Had he not been "a pansy," his parents would still be together.

The problems between Alan's parents involved many aspects of their adult relationship; different attitudes about children was only one of them. But all Alan could hear was that he was to blame. Visits with his father were very painful. Not only did Alan believe that he caused his parents' unhappiness, but also he was sure his father could never love him the way he was. Alan felt sad and defeated and did not know where to turn for help. His unhappiness deepened until his parents decided to seek counseling for their boy. How much suffering might have been avoided if Alan had not heard his mother and father arguing about him?

FRED

In some cases, a parent actually does leave the home because of a child. Children in this situation need special help to understand that there are some parents who do not know how to love their children, and who feel angry and overwhelmed by the responsibilities children bring. Even in these painful instances, we can try to find gentle ways to be honest. We might say something like "Daddy just doesn't feel ready to be a father right now, but that's a grown-up problem for Daddy to work out." What every child needs is constant reassurance that *he* or *she is lovable,* no matter how one parent acts. If we can help children understand that they are lovable just the way they are, we can help them become loving parents themselves, no matter what they've lived through. What an important job for any of us to undertake!

SUMMARY

- Every child has some feelings of responsibility and guilt related to the divorce, which in some cases even carries into their adult lives.

- Children need to be reassured repeatedly that they are not the reason for the divorce.

- It is best to prevent children from witnessing *any* arguments by the parents about the children.

CHAPTER 13

THE ONE-PARENT HOME

CLARE

When one parent moves out, a place as familiar as home can feel very strange. Here's how it seemed to some families:

> Kathy was eight years old when her parents divorced. "I remember lying on my bed," she told me, "looking around at the things in my room. Everything looked a little weird. I had a stuffed bear I'd taken to bed with me every night since I was two. Now he felt lumpy. After a few months I changed things around and put up some new posters on the wall. But home was never really the same after Daddy moved out."

One boy who spoke with me was ten when his parents divorced. On the day their father was to move out, the rest of the family visited friends. He and his sister had agreed beforehand that they would rather not watch their dad pack and move his things. "When we came back," Ralph told me, "the house seemed so much bigger. I thought Dad really took a lot of things with him."

Ralph's father actually packed only two suitcases with some clothing and a few books, no more than he had taken with him on any number of business trips. What was gone and making the house seem bigger and emptier to Ralph was, of course, his dad.

> "Every night since I can remember, my father read to me before I went to sleep," Michael said. "Now that he lives someplace else, how will I ever be able to fall asleep?" From the time Michael was a small baby, his dad enjoyed the hour before his bedtime playing with Michael or reading to him. As Michael's father commented, "It was the only time we had to be together each day. We started out with bedtime stories, and even after Michael learned to read we kept it up." When Michael's dad was away for some reason, his mother would read a story and that was fine. But after the separation Michael became particularly upset at bedtime and had trouble falling asleep.
>
> "I know how Michael felt," his father told me. "I really missed that time, too. It was a time for us to feel close and talk about things. It was a big help that Michael could talk about what was upsetting him. I decided to tape some stories for Michael, books I'd always planned to read with him, like *Treasure Island* and *Huck Finn*. I started each tape by saying I'd like to be with him reading this in person, but that we'd talk about it when we saw each other on the weekend.
>
> "I think sharing this with Michael helped a little. It made him understand that I missed some of the same things he did, and at least he heard the story, and he heard my voice."

No matter which parent leaves, it is natural for children to worry and feel that they have "lost" that parent. Michael must have found great reassurance in his dad's voice

—reassurance that his father was somewhere, that they would have times together and that his father still loved him.

> "I used to get upset when one of my children would remind me about the way their mother did something I was trying to do," Doug told me. "For the longest time I heard those statements as criticism that what I was doing wasn't good enough. Then I realized that I was trying to do things the way their mother did. When I made meals, instead of cooking something that I was good at, I'd try to make something their mother had cooked that we all liked. I would become frustrated and angry when things didn't turn out the way I planned. After a while, though, I got a lot more comfortable being myself and doing the things *I* was good at doing."

Sometimes children will get upset about seemingly small things: "Mommy cuts my sandwich in triangles, not squares. I can't eat a sandwich in squares." Or "I never wear those socks with my running shoes. I *can't* run in those socks!" It takes a while to feel comfortable about someone doing things in a new way. Since most children rely on established routines, keeping in mind that adjustment takes time can go a long way in helping a child feel secure.

Another father, Jack, who had custody of his two sons, told me: "When one of my sons would say something about how their mother did something, I would hear, 'And if it wasn't for you, she'd still be here.' I'd feel guilty and angry and very helpless."

FRED

Many parents talked to me about those kinds of feelings. Some told me they learned to say something like "That's true; I don't do some things the way Mommy does. We all do things a little differently." Sometimes when children say, "That's not the way Daddy reads this story" or "Mommy always has an apple for my lunch box," they are really saying that they miss the absent parent and wish they could be together as a family. A few parents told me about children missing things a parent never did at all.

> "Kathy is a wonderful mother to our two children," a divorced father said. "She is very creative and always thinks of the most enjoyable things to do. I don't know how she does it, but she'll be baking cookies for the PTA, building a model plane with one son and making a product map of Africa with the other—*all* at the same time.
>
> "The down side of that picture is that while all of this was going on, not much else was being done. The house was often in chaos. It was not unusual for a sneaker or a math book to be 'lost' for a few days. I'm very organized, and it was one of the differences that made our being married very difficult for me.
>
> "One afternoon when the boys were staying with me, we were getting ready to play tennis. I had gotten some new laces for Ned's sneakers. His old ones had so many knots in them they could no longer be tied. We were running late, and I couldn't remember where I'd put the laces. Ned was growing impatient as I looked, and he said, 'If Mom were here, she'd know where to find them.' There was a minute of silence, and then we all laughed very hard."

That father's story reminded me of another friend's experience. The Christmas after her husband died she was putting a Christmas tree in its stand, something she had done each holiday. She was having a lot of trouble with the tree. First, it leaned too far to the right, then to the left; she couldn't get the tree to stand straight. "I was getting more and more frustrated," she told me. "I told myself that if Joe were here, he'd have the tree up in two minutes." But in fact it had always been she who was capable in these situations. She could fix all sorts of things, while Joe never could. "I miss Joe so much," she told me. "It feels like everything would be easier if he were still here."

Grown-ups and children do feel like that sometimes, particularly in situations where we feel we have little or no choice about what is happening to us. Divorce is one of those times when almost everyone is likely to feel at the mercy of circumstance. For children, there is a magical element to love for a parent: Mommy can do *everything*. *Nothing* bad can happen to me as long as Daddy is here. When our children talk this way about us, it makes us smile, for we know that we can't do half of what they imagine. But these feelings help them to feel safe.

Yet, as we know, a child's positive feelings toward the absent parent can be hard for the remaining parent to tolerate. "I spend a whole week," one mother told me, "planning a perfect weekend with my son. I don't want him thinking about his dad all the time." A father put it this way: "I felt so angry after my wife and I separated I didn't want anyone to say anything good about her." Even though it's hard to separate adult feelings about divorce from children's feelings, it's something children need from us so that they can feel that the *family* will continue even if the marriage ends.

CLARE

Children of divorcing parents talk of many ways their home life changes. Sometimes, when each parent has had different expectations from their children, a good deal changes in the household routine. "Ted always wanted supper ready by six o'clock. We haven't had dinner at that time since he left." A house with one parent gets its rhythm from that parent. We help children become comfortable with these new rhythms if we encourage them to express how they are experiencing these changes and what they feel about them.

Often the remaining parent will become permissive even when he or she had never been before. One woman told me, "When Seth and I decided to divorce, I felt that we had stripped our children of everything that was important to them." Parents who share this mother's feeling sometimes attempt to "make it up" by easing up on accustomed discipline. While this is a perfectly understandable reaction on the part of parents, it does not help the children. Since divorce is a time of great confusion for children, helpful limits become even more crucial.

> "It seemed to me that my children had had such a rough time with our divorce," one father said. "Not just the separation, but living through the difficulties of the year before we separated. I figured that we should take a vacation from stress for a while.
>
> "What I ended up doing was taking all the rules away. I didn't want to hassle anyone about anything. It didn't take long for that plan to unravel. After a few days of meals on demand, television until ten o'clock and messy rooms, it was obvious that everyone was feeling worse, not better."

Most children feel more secure when they have a predictable routine. It can become an anchor during the change, when their inner world seems so unpredictable.

Sometimes, for economic reasons, a divorce can force a change in daily routine. A mother might find it necessary to work away from home for the first time. A father might find himself suddenly the principal, or sole caregiver. If this occurs where one parent has always been at home and available to a child, the change can prove dramatic.

"For me," Gretchen said, "the hardest thing to get used to was not having my mom around so much. She's an artist and, until my older brother was born, worked in an office. Since then she'd always painted at home. I used to like coming home from school and seeing her at her easel. Whenever she asked me about a painting she'd just finished, I knew she really listened to what I thought.

"After the divorce, we needed more money than Mom could earn at home. She tried working at home for almost a year, but wasn't able to cover all the expenses. So she found a job at an advertising agency, which kept her away from seven-thirty in the morning until dinner. Coming home and having no one there was very lonely."

FRED

Most mothers told me they, too, would have preferred keeping the predivorce routines.

"I had always planned to go back to work eventually," one said. "I'm a bookkeeper and supervised an entire department of a large company downtown. I was proud of my work and always thought I'd be a working mother. After our son was born, I kept putting off going back until I realized I'd rather be home with him. After he went to school, I found I still wasn't ready to go back. I enjoyed my time with him, and it seemed to me that he needed me almost as much as when he was a baby.

"After my divorce, I stayed home one more year, but we simply couldn't meet the expenses without my working. I miss not being with him after school. When I was a child, I never went home to an empty house, and I can't bear to think of him doing that either."

Some parents told me about after-school programs at school or in community centers, programs for children whose parents work. These programs could be very helpful; children need to be in some responsible person's care when their parents are away. That person needs to be someone sensitive to the things children need: a place to play, a place to work on some creative activity, and quiet space where children can read or just sit quietly and think. But I believe the most important resources children can have are the grown-ups themselves—adults who care enough to listen when children feel ready to play and talk about the important events in their lives.

SUMMARY

- No matter which parent leaves, it is natural for children to feel that he or she has "lost" that parent.

- Divorce is a time of great confusion for children, and helpful limits are even more crucial at this time.

- Most children feel better when they have a predictable routine. It can become an anchor during the change, when their inner world seems so unpredictable.

- No one parent can be everything to everyone. It's always best when the custodial parent acts naturally and doesn't make unrealistic demands upon herself or himself.

CHAPTER 14

WHEN DIVORCE MEANS MOVING TO A NEW HOME

CLARE

The parent who moves to a new place after a separation has a great many things to consider. Along with the personal adjustments to be made, he or she must create a new, second family home. Even such practical choices as where to live and how to arrange the available space will have some effect on the children. Unfortunately, new living arrangements are often made quickly or determined by a greatly reduced budget.

"When Ellen and I separated, I had two days to find someplace to live," Richard said. "I wasn't thinking too clearly, and I made some quick decisions only to have to change them soon after. A friend with whom I'd shared a lot, particularly during the months leading up to the separation, offered me an apartment over his garage. I felt quite close to him, although the rest of the family knew him less well.

"There were two problems with this living arrangement that I'd never thought about. The house was forty-eight miles from Ellen and the children. This may not seem like a great distance, but it was just enough to make it difficult for me to be with the children as much as I would have liked.

"I think that many things would have been smoother if we could have spent shorter periods of time together several times a week; if I had spent an hour or two with the kids, say working on their homework or just having dinner. But with that long drive every night, I just couldn't work in enough midweek visits. On the weekends, when there was more time, we all felt some pressure to fit things in.

"The other reason I needed to make a change had to do with *whom* I lived. My friend had two children almost the same age as mine. The first few times the kids came to my place were very tense. Finally my son Jack told me, 'You just went and found yourself a whole new family.' My children felt like they had been replaced.

"My first reaction to Jack's remark was that he was overreacting, but I could see how he might think that, that there was an element of truth in his statement. What I liked best about living there was that there was a family next door. We ate meals together or spent evenings watching TV and I think that 'borrowing' my friend's family was making me feel less lonely.

"Once I realized that, I knew I had to make other arrangements. Together, the kids and I talked about what might work best for all of us. We really shared a lot during that experience. I think they understand now that I put them ahead of anything else. I just wasn't able to think that clearly in the beginning.

"Finally, we did find a place, small because that was all I could afford, but close enough for me to visit during the week or for them to come here. It's a lot better all around."

Adequate living space at an affordable price seems to be a growing problem for all families. In divorce, the difficulties are often greater because the ideal arrangement is two homes, each large enough to afford space and privacy for nearly the same number of people. The reality, however, is that few families can afford such a housing situation.

"The towns within a commuting distance from my work are very expensive," one woman said. "And the city—well, rents there are out of sight. I am a graphic designer for a small, family-owned company. My salary isn't too great, but it's as much as I can expect in my field. At the time of the divorce, Nick and I decided that the kids would live with him. He has more money, works in his own business one mile from the house and is in a much better position to take care of them day-to-day.

"The hardest thing for me was to find a place that I could afford, yet big enough for both kids to have personal space. I wanted them to enjoy visiting.

"When one man in my office decided to move out West he offered me his small rent-controlled apartment —just one large room. When the kids first saw it, their faces dropped. I knew exactly what they were thinking because I shared their disappointment.

"We sat down and I explained the realities of our choices; that this apartment was the biggest place I could afford and still have money for the other things we needed. I asked them what they would like to do to make the apartment feel more like home. They each made lists, and I did some drawings of how those things would fit in the space. With each set of drawings, we made some revisions and eventually found a way to fit almost everything we needed into that little space.

"With my brother's help we created places for each of us to enjoy some privacy. My son has his bed on a five-foot platform, which has room for books and a radio, and is high enough off the ground so that no one sees or bothers him. My daughter has a soft Japanese mattress called a futon that she rolls up during the day. Because she wanted an area for her crafts projects—many of which we work on together—part of her space is under the platform.

"Every now and then we feel like we're stepping on one another, but we're all very proud of the apartment because we figured it out together and it works well for us."

FRED

Children can learn to feel at home in a new, strange space, especially if they're able to have a place, no matter how small, for keeping familiar things—a special blanket, some old toys, or even an ongoing creative project of some kind. Most parents can find a small place like that, even in a one-room apartment.

People say, "Children are so adaptable, they can adjust to anything." Children *do* tend to be adaptable, but that doesn't mean "anything goes." I was talking with a friend of mine, a child psychologist, who told me about a divorced father who had his son sleep in bed with him, while his daughter shared a bed with his girlfriend. This father had the best intentions, but the children were upset and confused by the arrangement. Each child would have been better off, my friend told me, with a separate place to sleep, even if it were only a sleeping bag on the floor. And then there are ways to make a new home look welcoming.

"I was real nervous when I went to see my dad's new home," one girl told me. "I couldn't imagine what it would be like. I remember some of my friends saying that their divorced parents' houses were weird because they were so different. My first visit to Dad's place was something I didn't want to do, and I hoped it would go quickly.

"But Dad's house was nothing like I'd imagined. He had pictures of the family all around the house—even one with Mom in it. In his bedroom, he had framed some of our schoolwork. I had been dreading seeing a place that had nothing to do with us, but all those things made me feel at home."

That girl's dad felt his family was so important that he wanted reminders of them all around him. He told me that his marriage, from which his family was created, might be over, but his family was not. "I couldn't see going around cutting my wife's pictures out of the photographs of the family. We'll have new ones from this time, but I don't want to be left with only mental pictures of my children when they were growing up."

CLARE

Almost every parent I spoke with wanted to smooth the way for their children. Very often I would hear, "I know my kids are hurting. If only there was some way for me to take on some of their hurt." It is natural for loving parents to want to protect their children, but sometimes we simply can't do that. There are times when protecting them doesn't really help at all. One divorced father tells how he learned this lesson best from his own son.

"My son was thirteen when his mother and I divorced. I knew from my own feelings and those of my divorced friends, that every parent who is separated from a child wants the time spent with that child to be special. I knew also, however, that times with my son should not turn into holidays. But it's very hard to find the balance, particularly when everything feels so new. Whenever we got together, I inevitably tried to make things as easy as I could for him. I always had everything ready before he arrived. While he was with me I'd have his bed made before he finished brushing his teeth. I'd make his favorite breakfasts, and while he was eating, do the dishes. I never wanted hassles over chores, so I just did everything myself. It was finally my son who pointed out to me what didn't feel right about all of this. He said, 'Dad, it doesn't feel *real* when we're together. I feel like a guest, not like I really belong here.'"

"He only wanted to feel at home and all my fussing was making it impossible for him to settle in. By taking away all the rules we'd followed for years, by trying to 'protect' him—and myself—from any disagreements or discomfort, I was making it harder, *not* easier, for him."

FRED

Taking some responsibility can make children feel good about themselves. When we give our children reasonable things to be responsible for, it helps them grow into being independent and more responsible for themselves. It's natural for parents to feel that a divorce puts too many responsibilities on children, and sometimes it does. But taking other important responsibilities away from children will not help them feel capable and strong. Children can often share responsibility for maintaining routines of the past, and these routines may be a comfort for many children; they can feel that some things continue even though other things change. As they try new, and often scary things, responsibilities from the past—taking care of their own things, helping with the house—can bring confidence and security.

"I help. I'm important. I can do many things myself." Children need these feelings as they grow.

CLARE

It is easy to take for granted things that may make some children feel intimidated. Leaving a place as comfortable and secure as home is a little unsettling for most everyone, but for younger children, an unfamiliar neighborhood can be very frightening. "Who will I play with? Who are these people? What if I get lost?" All of these are questions that can trouble children in a new place, even if they are only going for a short visit. One mother I know spent her two children's first few visits helping them feel at home in her new surroundings. She introduced her children to the grocer and the druggist. She taught them safety requirements important to her neighborhood. The corner didn't have a four-way stop; more cars rode down this street near suppertime. Having this information greatly reduced her children's fears and it wasn't long before the new place began to feel like home.

The telephone and written notes are wonderful ways to stay close to our children when we cannot be with them. When I travel, I talk with my family every day. Even a week can feel like a very long time to a child. Staying in touch between visits can help the parent who has moved out to maintain closeness.

"My parents got divorced when I was eight," one young woman told me. "It was my father who moved out. I'd spend weekends with him, but had no contact during the week. By about Wednesday I would start to imagine all kinds of awful things. We'd never discussed the arrangement, so I just assumed I wasn't supposed to talk to him except on the weekends. One time when Mom was out and I had a baby sitter, I just called him. I felt so much better. I still remember it."

Frequent contact, even by telephone, can help a child feel closer to an absent parent. It can greatly relieve any worries and allows a child to talk about the everyday things, some big, some small, that make up his or her life.

SUMMARY

- A parent who moves to a new place will have a great number of concerns, one of the most important being the necessity of creating a home in which the children feel comfortable.

- Establishing private space, consistent routine, and responsibility (within the child's capabilities) will help children to feel secure in their new surroundings.

- Help your children familiarize themselves with a new neighborhood: show them where the stores are, introduce them to neighbors and merchants, alert them to any possible dangers.

- Telephone calls and written notes are wonderful ways to stay close to our children when we cannot be with them.

CHAPTER 15

ESTABLISHING COMFORTABLE VISITING ROUTINES

FRED

Transitions are a large part of all that we're talking about. In fact, transitions are a large part of living. Most of us need time, patience and a lot of love as we adjust to new ways of life. Divorces often mean children have to adjust to a new home, and that can be a difficult transition for anyone. For one sixteen-year-old, for instance, the idea of visiting her father seemed "crazy." As she put it, "People don't *visit* their fathers, they live with their father and visit museums."

This girl's father lived in a hotel to begin with, and she didn't like the atmosphere. It seemed to her that all there was in this new "home" was a bed, a bathroom, a telephone and a TV set. She remembers that the lamps were all nailed down to the tables, and she found that depressing.

"I remember thinking," she recalled, "that Dad would probably move back home any minute, because no matter how bad things got between him and my mother, living in that hotel had to be worse."

Eventually her father found a small apartment. It was comfortable and large enough for both her and her brother to have their own living space. During the first six months, the three of them spent time fixing it up. "At first," she told me, "I couldn't believe that I would ever feel comfortable there. It reminded me of the way I felt when I was five years old and I went to a school friend's house for the first time. Everything seemed strange and a little uncomfortable. But now I feel good there. It took all of us time, but it happened."

CLARE

In time, most visitation arrangements become routine and family members adjust to whatever agreements have been established. There are times, however, when parents and children find the need to be flexible about agreements. Even so, when both child and parent learn to count on these visits, making changes can be very difficult.

Pam was four when her parents divorced. The agreement arrived at by her parents included visits on alternate weekends. For the several years that Pam lived in the same city as her father, the agreement worked well. His remarriage and subsequent move to a suburban community fifteen minutes away coincided with changes in Pam's own social life. As with many teenagers, her weekends were becoming filled with school dances, play practices, or movie dates with her school friends. Pam's interest in seeing her father was as strong as ever, but visiting him meant feeling out of a social life. In one year, each school dance was scheduled on a weekend Pam was due to visit her father. When she asked to change her arrival from Friday evening to Saturday afternoon to attend the dances, Pam's father refused, insisting their visits were more important than a school dance.

Some parents, however, make such an effort to be accommodating to a child's schedule that their flexibility is misinterpreted.

Chris's parents separated when he was eight and his sister eleven. The visitation agreement between Chris's parents included school vacations with his father, particularly the months of July and August. The first summer Chris asked to spend one month at camp, as he had done the previous summer, and his father reluctantly agreed. His father missed the time with his son but believed Chris should have the same experiences his friends were having. As Chris and his sister grew older, their extracurricular activities increased, gradually cutting into time set aside for visits with their father until Christmas vacations were spent on school ski trips and both children were spending two months at summer camp.

Though motivated by the sincere desire to prevent the divorce from ruining his children's lives, Chris's father's efforts to be accommodating were eventually interpreted by his children as indifference. He wasn't able to communicate the pain he felt about missing his time with them.

There are times when the demands from either side feel too great. Once again, talking can help. Regular contact with both parents is very important. While visitation agreements need not be followed to the letter, activities that seriously interfere with one parent's time should be carefully controlled. It helps everyone if both parents can be flexible.

When Robbie ended his marriage he was sure that his decision to divorce was best for him and the family. He left their home and two children and found an apartment only a five-minute drive away. He thought that being physically near to his children would help maintain the emotional closeness they had shared at home. Robbie was dismayed to learn that most of the time the five minutes felt like five years. His children were accessible only at hours appointed for visitation, and the routine details that made their former relationship so close were gone. He felt the loss very deeply.

The noncustodial parents I talked with all spoke of the intense feeling of loss specifically related to the children. One mother recalled months of feeling totally worthless as she adjusted to living without her two sons. "How can I have any worth as a person?" she asked herself, "if I can't even be a mother to my own sons." A father spending the first months away from his son and daughter told us that he felt an emptiness so enormous that he "imagined himself a shell, not a person." These parents, like many others, took great comfort from their relationship with their children and felt lost without daily contact.

As one divorced father put it: "What I miss more than anything is the opportunity to bathe my son, hold him on my lap, read him a story and put him to bed."

FRED

How natural it is for noncustodial parents to experience intense feelings of loss! They have lost not only a spouse and a marriage, but a daily relationship with their children as well. Of course, most parents in this position feel sad. They may feel angry, as well. Others become deeply fearful about the well-being of their children. One father told me that for a long time he was sure he had ruined the lives of his whole family. He felt guilty and pessimistic about his children's chances for a happy future. All of these reactions are natural *human* responses to loss.

Loss can be disorienting, too.

One woman moved into an apartment not far from her family. About six months after she moved away from the home she had shared with her husband and two sons, she began to feel restless all the time she was not at work in her office. Many nights she would wander through department stores, looking at things she would never need, until the closing bell rang. She felt trapped inside her apartment alone but too edgy to be with friends. One Friday night she came home from work, went to bed and did not get up until Monday morning, when it was time to go to work again.

Listlessness, depression—"numbness," as one father put it—are all reactions that divorced parents have mentioned many times. They have to be endured, and it may be of some help to realize that they're a usual part of the healing process. That process tends to go in stops and starts: It's common to feel much better for a time, only to experience a recurrence of the sad and restless feelings. These sudden bouts of recurring loneliness are *not* necessarily setbacks.

Many people can be comforted by friends and relatives, but others can't—at least not for a while. It seems we have to begin to accept our own feelings before we can share them with people we trust. Even then, sharing our feelings may seem like an imposition. But when a good friend offers to listen, it can really help to talk—even if words are hard to find.

CLARE

Visits with a noncustodial parent affect each person in the family, the child or children and both divorced parents. The times preceding and following a visit are times of adjustment for everyone. Children often feel restless or upset. The parent with custody must help prepare every-one for a change and then work to reestablish a routine.

And the noncustodial parent must adjust to the feelings of loneliness and loss that reoccur after each visit.

"The first few months after my legal separation were the hardest," Pat told me. "I felt I could never relax. My children were eight and ten. Like most kids, they would have preferred that Ed and I stay together. The night before their weekend visits with their father were always difficult. They couldn't get their homework done. They got into arguments with each other or with me. For a time I wondered if they really wanted to see their father.

"Sunday nights were just as bad. They usually came into the house not speaking to each other. It seems they never got *any* homework done over the weekend and weren't able to settle down and do it in the evening. I couldn't imagine what was going on at Ed's house."

From Ed's perspective, events of the weekend were equally disconcerting.

"All week long I waited to see the kids," Ed explained. "When you're not with your children every day, you don't remember any of the annoying things, just the good things. I would be tremendously excited to see them and filled with plans for what we would do.

"But instead of seeing the happy faces I had so eagerly anticipated, I was usually greeted with, at most, a glum 'hello.' Both children were angry with each other. Sometimes they were unwilling to give up their scrapping for the entire evening. The weekend was rarely as warm and friendly as I'd hoped. It was a difficult time."

Pat and Ed had pretty good communication about the children throughout the separation and eventual divorce. When they arranged to meet and talk about the visits, they realized that each parent was having a similar experience.

"At first I blamed Ed and he blamed me," Pat said. "Our attitude was, 'What are *you* doing to make the kids act like that?' Of course, neither one of us was doing anything. All of our moods were coming from the upset of this new life we were getting used to. I resolved to be stricter with myself about keeping to our own routines of dinner, homework, and play and to be sure to save personal, quiet times to share with each of the children a day or so before a visit. Ed tried to make his expectations for the visits a little more realistic. It's hard though, when we only have short periods of time with our children. Naturally, any parent would want that time to be happy and trouble-free."

"All of this coming and going has finally become routine," Ed remarked. "We are all much more comfortable with everything. Like so many aspects of divorce, it takes time, love and a big effort."

SUMMARY

- Transitions, though a large part of living, can be difficult. Children need time, patience and a lot of love as they learn to adjust to new ways of life.

- There are times when parents and children need to be flexible about established visitation agreements, but always with an awareness that, no matter what the social responsibilities in a person's life, children and parents need to spend time together.

- By sharing our feelings of loss and anger with those we trust, we set a good example for our children.

- Visits with the noncustodial parent can be disruptive and will affect every family member. Preparation and the adherence to routine can help everyone make the transition easier.

CHAPTER 16

HOLIDAY TIMES CAN BE TIMES OF SPECIAL STRESS

FRED

I've read and heard that many couples wait to separate until after the first of the year. As I talked with some families about this, I understood that they were delaying the actual separation to preserve one last holiday memory for their children—and for themselves.

> One couple had more or less worked out the details of their separation during the summer, but as they talked about telling the children, both agreed to make the break in January. They wanted their children to have one more Hanukkah, one more Thanksgiving, together as a family.
>
> The children's mother voiced another thought, too: "I think both of us also wondered how *we* would manage with the holidays. There were so many issues to think about. Which parent would be with the children? And when? Both of us had to face the prospect of being alone at least part of the time. It was just too frightening."

CLARE

It is not at all surprising that a couple might wait for a favorite family holiday to pass before going ahead with the final separation; often there is a great deal of special consideration involved in holiday planning. Some divorcing couples remember holidays together as the happy times of their marriage. Other parents worry that a divorce deprives their children of the fullest celebratory experience—a "greeting card" holiday setting—even when the family doesn't have particularly happy holiday memories.

Holidays can be difficult for many people, but following any separation or family loss they can be particularly confusing and painful. For some families, old conflicts resurface, but for many I spoke with, new situations gave rise to new ways of celebrating, making everyone more comfortable.

> "I won't tell you for one minute that I wouldn't rather be celebrating a different Thanksgiving this year," Sam told me. "For the last ten years my ex-wife and I celebrated the holidays with my family, either here in New Mexico or at my sister's place in Arizona. It was a time for us to see each other's kids, catch up on family news and have an old-fashioned family reunion. Now that we're divorced, the kids will spend Thanksgiving with their mother and some of her college friends about a hundred miles from my sister's place. Then I'll get the kids on Friday, and we'll spend our time together while Sally takes the weekend for herself."

One measure of how important holiday traditions are is the difficulty we have in establishing new ways to celebrate when our lives change. Sam and Sally's solution was good for everyone. Each parent shared part of the holiday with the children because they were able to accept the fact that there was nothing really sacred about a Thursday in November, that the holiday was a time for family and festivity. Sam had a few sad moments that day, but, as he said, "The children felt a lot better that Sally and I could work out something that considered everybody's feelings. They got to spend time with both parents, their aunt and cousins and their grandparents. It wasn't *ideal* for anybody, but it was pretty good for everyone."

FRED

I believe children in most situations want to share the holidays with both parents. When parents live near each other, they have sometimes divided the day in half. Other parents celebrate with the children on different days. In some ways, this means "doubling" the holidays for the children, and that can mean doubling the stimulation as well. We need to remember that there's only so much children can take.

Even parents who are not divorcing have found how easily their young children can be overwhelmed by too much all at once—too many toys at Christmas, too many children at a birthday party. Divorces can make this problem worse, particularly with all the other feelings that are stirred up under the surface and with the tendency many divorced parents have to become competitive over who gives their children the most.

One mother, who really couldn't afford it, bought each one of her children eight of the best presents she could find. It took her almost a year to pay off the bills. And yet, when they came back elated from their father's house after their time with him, her first thought was, "What did *he* give the children?" It turned out that their father had made them a favorite breakfast: pancakes with syrup, a reminder of a trip they'd once made to Vermont. Most parents find sooner or later that material gifts rarely represent affection in a child's mind. Sharing love and time are the kinds of gifts children remember.

CLARE

One couple worked out a plan that reduced holiday gift pressures for the whole family, including grandparents.

"For the first few years after the divorce, Dan and I couldn't agree on anything. There were gifts he thought were fine that I didn't want the children to have. One that sticks in my mind is a skateboard. He lives in a place where children can use a skateboard without fear of traffic or other dangers. I'm in an apartment on a street with cars, buses and taxicabs. Skateboards terrified me," Pat said.

"For a time it seemed that he only bought the children things that would annoy me," she went on. "Of course, that isn't true. He thought of gifts that fit their life-style with him, and I thought of gifts that fit their life-style with me. Many times it seemed to me that my gifts were dull and his were all fun.

"After three years of feeling upset about this, I sat down and talked with Dan about how I felt. He also had concerns about the disparity in the kinds of gifts we were giving and the impressions we were making on the children as to their parents' values. As Dan saw it, the kids were just as likely to see him as frivolous. He didn't want that any more than I wanted them to think I was the wet blanket. The plan we devised helped us all feel a lot better. Now, over Thanksgiving, each child makes a list of the things he wants. Dan and I get together and talk about the lists—sometimes adding things we think they need. Then we divide it up and agree on who will give what. Under this plan, I would even give a skateboard—provided they kept it at Dan's place and used it in a safe place."

Any plan that encourages cooperation, rather than competition, can help families avoid a great deal of upset at holiday time.

No matter how an individual family arranges the holiday schedule, it's important for both parents to make an effort to allow the children time for contact with each parent. That goes for grandparents as well. So much of our connection to family traditions takes root at this time.

Old memories may be powerful. Perhaps it is inevitable that both parents will feel some sadness during the holidays. The children may as well. Developing alternative ways of celebrating these times is one of the ways that parents teach children to adapt to new situations and to view things from different people's points of view.

"I was nine when I spent the first Christmas without my parents together," one girl told me. "The first Christmas was the worst. My friends whose parents are divorced say that the same was true for them, too. One kid said, 'Boy, are you lucky—two Christmases—twice as many presents.' That made me so mad. I'd rather have no Christmas and both my parents," she said with some sadness in her voice.

"After a while I got more used to the whole thing. One year I had Christmas Eve with Mom and her family and then Christmas Day with Dad and his. The next year we'd switch to the other way. I'll never really forget that first day without both parents, but I've grown a lot through those times. My parents made sure I had one whole day with each of them. I had time with both grandparents and with my cousins, too. We're all close in a nice way, my family. We never got cut off from anyone. I think my parents really helped that happen. It's one of the things I really appreciate about them."

FRED

We can always expect holiday times to bring us hardships as well as pleasures. They're almost sure to bring us feelings of loss even as they bring us new joys to remember later on. Grandparents die, grandchildren are born; in family gatherings there are times of anger as well as times of love. That's the way it is for all families, whether there's been a divorce or not. And as these vignettes of family life have suggested, there are no gifts we can *buy* that will enable children to grow healthily through a divorce. The only gift capable of doing that is the gift of ourselves when we can offer it freely, truly, and with love.

SUMMARY

- Holidays can be especially stressful and call for the creation of new traditions to fit new circumstances. Whenever possible, ways should be found that allow children to share these special times with each of their parents.

- "Doubling" the holidays can mean doubling the stimulation. Parents should refrain from competing with each other over who gives the children the most and take care not to overwhelm. Sometimes sharing love and time is the greatest gift a parent can give.

- Children and grandparents need to spend time together, especially during holidays when family traditions are so important.

- Developing alternative ways of celebrating holiday times is one of the ways that parents can teach children to adapt to new situations and to view things from other people's points of view.

CHAPTER 17

CONCLUSION

Many of the stages and most of the feelings we've discussed within the context of divorce are actually common, in one form or another, to all children. Fears of separation, the need for independence, feelings of guilt and anxiety, are all part of the growing each of us does throughout our lives. Divorce, like any great loss, is apt to intensify these and other troubling feelings. It is important to remember that children resolve these feelings about divorce in their own special ways. There is simply no right or wrong way to accomplish this. Among the valuable things we learned from those who so generously shared their experiences with us, this was perhaps the most striking. No two children will experience a divorce or any of its life-altering consequences in the same way, nor will they follow the same timetable in its resolution.

The separation children experience in divorce is similar in many ways to a child's separation from a mother or primary care giver. Upset feelings don't only come with great intensity at the beginning, and then get settled forever and ever. Rather the feelings of loss are part of a continuous chain of connected feelings. The sad and angry feelings return in varying degrees of intensity at different times in a person's life. Remembering this helped many parents we spoke with accept the times these feelings occurred as part of the normal fabric of growing through —and with—divorce.

There were times when hearing the divorce experiences of these parents and children was very sad. Most had gone through some very hard times with divorce. Even in those instances where divorce had occurred long before our discussion, the emotions ran high and the experiences were vivid. But, on balance, sharing these stories has left us feeling positive and optimistic. For all of the difficult times children experience when their parents divorce, so many have grown through their experiences and remained strong and capable.

As with most parents, those who divorce would rather their children never feel sad or angry, frightened or alone. But all of these feelings have an inevitable and valuable place in each of our lives.

Children will often adjust to new situations with stops and starts, sometimes placing heavy demands on themsleves. But with support and encouragement they will learn how to ask for help, learn to trust a new world of adult strangers—a teacher, the school nurse, the librarian, the sports coach—and much of this on their own, learning in the process to trust in their own reserves.

Children whose parents divorce can learn to tap sources of inner strength that will help them through other difficult experiences. Certainly parents and other caring adults can and do make an enormous difference. But for many children, the greatest strengths come from within themselves. As they accepted the reality of their parents' breakup, many children learned to accept the reality of other difficult situations, became more realistic about relationships, and grew to understand that they can experience a great loss and emerge whole and happy again.

"I thought the hurt would never go away," one girl said, "but after a while I felt a little bit better. Then I felt almost normal again. Now I know that nothing will ever make me feel quite *that* bad ever again. Best of all, I know that no matter how sad I may feel, *I will feel better*. That makes me feel strong and good about myself."

The pages that follow are from a book written by a young boy as a gift for his father two years after his parents' divorce. It is, we think the most fitting conclusion to this book, a last word, as it were, on a child who has grown through the experience of his parents' divorce.

"TO MY DAD . . ."

This Book is
Dedicated to Dad,
Mom, Paul, and
a little to Holly

When I Arrived

I came out crying like a baby because I was a baby. In fact I was a nine pound baby. I was a twenty-three-inch little squirt. I was the first kid in the family so it must have changed my parents' life a great deal, like they probably couldn't go out on any special dinners without taking me along with them. I started to walk when I was seventeen months old. I said my first words when I was eleven months. I loved Heinz baby food. But the statistics don't matter, I'm in this world now and I'm glad that I am.

My Folks

I love my folks more than anything in the world. They have been separated for two and a half years, but it doesn't bother me very much. I live with my mother and I go to New York every other weekend to see my dad, but sometimes he'll take us (my sister and me) for more than two days, like he'll take us for Spring Vacation. This year I went to Dad's for Christmas, but next year I will probably stay at Mom's. I do all the things other kids do, if not more. There are some good things about divorce, like I get two Christmases. But I have two parents that I think are just great, and I'm lucky to have that much.

My Sister

I have but one nine-year-old sister. Her name is Holly. We have a lot of fights that don't mean much to me. I like her in ways and I don't like her in ways. She does me a lot of favors that I appreciate, but sometimes she gets a little on the pain side. I guess all brothers and sisters have problems when they are young, and then when they get older they become like friends. Deep down I guess I like her. She's my sister and I guess I should like her, and I guess I do.

My Grandparents

I have six wonderful grandparents. I'll start with Grandma and Grandpa Gyde (on my father's side). They live in upper Michigan. Grandpa retired in May of '73, I think. Their house was almost done last time I saw it, it's a really keen place. I think it has three bedrooms, with a trailer out back, that I wouldn't mind staying in myself. The property has about three quarters of an acre, and it's about one half of a mile from a small town. There is a lake about three quarters of a mile down the road that we can go fishing in. (Grandpa loves to fish.) On my mother's side I have four grandparents: Grandma and Grandpa Engleman, and great Grandma and Grandpa Taylor. The Englemans, who live in Michigan, are going to retire sometime this year. They are going to raise and race horses, with my great Uncle Perry.

Last but not least, my Grandma and Grandpa Taylor. They live in Arizona. I've only been to visit once and all I can say is that it's hot. I got sick when we were there. We went to a restaurant and we were in line for our food and all of the sudden I got sick. I love my grandparents very much and I think they are very generous when we are around, as if we never see them. I think grandparents are great and I wish everyone had as many as I do.

Pets

I can count nine pets that we've had. They are as follows: Snapper (mine), Wilton and Stamford (Stamford is known as Stupid Stick, and they are both Holly's), and Pawcatuck (she is both of ours). My mom doesn't like cats very much, but we've had four. We got our first two when we just moved to New Canaan and some people wanted to give away their kittens. We took two. I called mine Snapper and Holly called hers Wilton. They were both tiger-like and were real playful when they were young. They're not alive right now and I don't want to say how. Holly got Stamford for her birthday and he is now a father of four. He's in his older years now, but he's as nice as he was in the beginning. We got Pawcatuck around two and one half months ago. She is a playful little devil. Getting her was a real surprise. We got her when my mom came back from Watch Hill, Rhode Island. Up there a man had plenty of kittens and Mom decided to bring one home. She stays in our bathroom downstairs, but she comes out a lot.

Cecil our dog is great. He is a Weimaraner and Labrador Retriever. He is ten years old but he plays like he is three. He can do a lot of tricks. He is great when we need him. Santa, who was my uncle Mark's dog, once stayed at our old house for the summer. She died from too much heat when it was 102 degrees out. Santa was a Saint Bernard. Pie, who is a Golden Retriever and Irish Setter, is three and one half, I think. He is clumsy sometimes, and sometimes a pain. But otherwise he is very lovable, and I like him just as much as all of our pets.

We've also had a pony and a bird. Christy, our pony that we used to have, was frisky sometimes, and we had to sell her when we moved. I really liked her and I used to ride her a lot. B.J. our bird was a parakeet. We had him for about three years. He is buried at our old house. We went for a vacation and when we got back we found him under my bed and he was dead. Everyone was very sad. I really like or liked all of my pets, and I'm glad my family puts up with them.

Family History

Family History is something that should be included in this book. One of my grandmothers is one-quarter American Indian. My great great great great grandmother was an Indian. My grandmother's great grandmother lived to be 102 years old. She was a half-breed. All my grandmother's side is from Beaver Dam, Kentucky. My Grandpa Engleman is from Russia. He is the eighth kid from eight. Five of his brothers and sisters died from tragedies which are: polio, fire, and muscular dystrophy. I think my family history is sad, but isn't everyone's?

Things We Do Together

We do a lot of nice things together. With my father we do everything that you can do in New York. Each time I visit we do something different, and I like everything that we do except that we take a lot of walks and sometimes I get a little tired. In Connecticut, with my mom, we go out a lot, like to dinner. Other times we do special things at home. I like everything we do together. But most of all we are together and that's what counts.

Where We Live

By the time you get this Dad, Mom and Paul will be married and since we have a new house we'll probably be living there. I don't know a ton about it but this is what I can tell you: It's on Oenoke Ridge; it has three bathrooms; and my room is to the left of the top of the stairs and I have a nice bath. The thing I like about the house is that there are a lot of crawl spaces. There's one where you take out part of a wall to get to it—it's like a secret passage. There isn't any attic but the crawl spaces make up for that. Our playroom will be over the garage. It's going to have to have a lot of work done on it. Mom and Paul have a lot of great ideas for it so I really think I'm going to like living there.

171

Family Traditions

Our family has pretty many family traditions. One of our best family traditions is getting up at six in the morning on Christmas to open our presents. We also get to open one present on Christmas Eve. We don't go to church very much at all. We get to stay up until midnight on New Year's Eve. On birthdays we get to choose what we want for dinner. I like most family traditions, but there are some that are a little dull.

What I've Learned From My Family

I have learned almost everything from my family. One thing is that when your parents are divorced they love you just as much as if they were married. My family has taught me manners, how to be friendly, how to be kind and to be nice to adults and do what they tell me to do. They have helped me become better at sports and they help me on homework and things like that. They teach me everything that they can outside of school. I could go on and on telling you what my family has taught me. I really do appreciate what my family has taught me because I have to learn sometime and they help me do that, now.

What My Family Means To Me—
Mainly *EVERYTHING*

My family is my whole life. It's something to look forward to when you come home from school. My family means comfort, warmth, and love. They give me respect and things that a kid really needs. My family means food, shelter, clothes, and to get a haircut or to get some candy when I want some. My family really does mean everything to me. What could mean more than a Family?

A Final Word

This hasn't been an every day cop-out job. It took a lot of hard thinking, and a heart for the words to come from. It has been a hard tough job to do, and to my father—who will have to take this for all of his presents for '73 because I didn't finish that rug I was working on—I hope that you and the rest of the family will treasure this for the rest of your lives.

APPENDIX

At any age we can feel empty—feel as if there's NOTHING—but if we find *one caring person* who will listen thoughtfully to how we feel, who will help us know how much we're loved, then our empty NOTHING can begin to change into an important SOMETHING. It takes time—sometimes lots of time—but it's worth it.

The following is a story about some of the things that have been bothering a child about divorce. It concerns an important turning point in that child's life. It's a story for an adult and child to read together—over and over.

Something out of nothing is possible only through love. That's what this story is all about. As you read it, as you talk about it, as you listen, it is a gift of love from you to your child.

Fred Rogers

"Nothing."

She couldn't keep the nothing in any longer. She had to tell somebody! But whom? Her mother seemed angry all the time. Her dad didn't live at home anymore. Sometimes she felt very lonely. But, when they would ask her what she thought, she usually said . . . "nothing."

Just then she thought she saw Mister Rogers—not on the television, but right outside her window. "Is there anything you'd like to tell me?" he seemed to be saying.

And she almost answered, "No. No, thank you. Nothing . . ." But instead of No, she said, "Yes, there's a lot I want to tell, but I don't know where to start." And Mister Rogers said, "Just start wherever you're thinking."

And right away she said, "My mom and dad don't love each other anymore. They told me they didn't, and they're going to get a . . .

"divorce."

As soon as she said it, she knew that Mister Rogers knew it was serious, because he sat down on a bench and said to her, "If you want to, come outside, and we'll talk about it." So she did.

"I need my mommy—but I need my daddy, too," she told Mister Rogers. And he said right away, "I'm sure you do."

"Some of the time I'm going to live with my mommy and some of the time I'm going to live with my daddy, and I'll have a bed at both places. I'll carry my Flopper with me wherever I go. But," she said, "I think Flopper would like it better if he could live in just one house."

"Divorce is sad," Mister Rogers said, "sad for everybody." And she said, "It's all kinds of sad: crying sad . . . and angry sad . . . and very, very quiet sad." They sat together for a long, long time and didn't say anything.

"Do you think maybe the whole divorce thing was somehow my fault?" she finally asked. But Mister Rogers helped her begin to believe that it wasn't. He helped her to understand that divorce was something grown-ups did and it wasn't their children's fault.

And then she remembered that her mom had said that, too, and her dad had said it, too. "Divorce is not the children's fault." But she guessed it took a while to understand it for sure.

"Isn't there anything I can do to change it all back to the way it used to be?" she finally asked Mister Rogers. "No, there isn't," he told her. "You didn't make the divorce happen, and you can't make it un-happen either. It's an unhappy thing, isn't it?" And she said, "It certainly is, but I'm glad I could talk about it with you." And she gave Mister Rogers a big hug.

Then she felt like telling about all the things that she and her mom like to do together . . . and all the things that she and her dad like to do together.

Mister Rogers said, "You can still have special times with your mom, and you can still have special times with your dad. Divorce doesn't change everything. It doesn't change the thing that's the most special of all. There's something

between you and your mom and between you and your dad
that's called love . . ."

That's really something, she kept thinking . . . *REALLY*

SOMETHING.

About the Authors

FRED MCFEELY ROGERS, known to millions of American families as "Mister Rogers" of *Mister Rogers' Neighborhood*, was born in 1928. He graduated from Rollins College with a B.A. in music composition and became a creator and producer of television programming for children. In addition, he found time to complete his theological studies at the Pittsburgh Theological Seminary and was ordained as a minister in the United Presbyterian Church. He also took the Masters program in Child Development at the University of Pittsburgh. The Rogers family—his wife, who is a concert pianist, and their two sons—live in Pittsburgh.

CLARE LYNCH O'BRIEN is a writer and educational consultant. She assisted in the development of the Emmy and Peabody award-winning children's television series, *Big Blue Marble,* for which she served as educational consultant and writer throughout its nine-year broadcast.

Ms. O'Brien met Fred Rogers in India in 1979 when they and two other television producers were guests of the Indian government for an exchange of ideas and experiences in children's television production. During this trip, Ms. O'Brien credits Fred Rogers with talking—and listening—her through this first long separation from her young family.

She lives in New York City with her husband and two children.